A basic guide to

Appreciating Wine

by J.B. Andersen

Published by Dorn Books
7101 York Ave So
Minneapolis, MN
55435

Creative Supervisor: Kenneth M. Nelson
Art Director: Sherry Reutiman
Illustrations: James Simondet

First Edition
First Printing 1979

ISBN 0-934070-04-0

Introduction

American wine drinkers are quietly staging a revolution. In increasing numbers they are becoming interested in a wide variety of wines, and in turn, they are introducing multitudes of their friends to wine.

At one time American wine drinkers fell into one of two categories: winos or snobs. Now, all kinds of people are enjoying wine at all sorts of occasions.

At the beginning of the 20th century, Americans consumed about 100 million gallons of wine annually. Today, nearly 400 million gallons are consumed, and by 1990 Americans will probably be drinking more than a billion gallons of wine a year.

Not only are we drinking more wine, but our tastes in wine are changing. Traditionally, sweet wines have been favored in the United States. Since 1960, however, Americans have become interested in the drier table wines. As a result, California winegrowers in particular have been steadily replacing old stock with grapes that are used to make the traditional European dinner wines. These new grapes have greatly improved the quality of our own domestic wines—where once all good wine had to be imported, fine domestic wines are now readily available at popular prices.

Why this increased consumption? Why the change in taste? What makes people become interested in wine? Why is more wine now served at parties, at cocktail time, and with meals?

One major factor in increased wine consumption in the United States is the interest certain large corporations now have in developing a wine market among Americans. Several corporations have purchased small wineries in California and launched massive advertising campaigns to promote their products. Yet this is only one reason for the great wine success story in America today.

Another factor is increased travel by Americans in Europe. Wine at meals is a custom far more common in European countries than in the United States. Every year, Italy and

France each produce more than two billion gallons of wine—making our annual production of 400 million gallons look paltry by comparison. When Americans who travel abroad return home, they often request the wines they were introduced to and enjoyed in Europe.

Many Americans have been introduced to wine by the sweet "pop" wines now on the market. After sipping the "pop" wines for several months, they usually decide to try something else. Gradually their tastes begin to change and they purchase other—usually drier—wines. They begin to try wine with food, and they are on their way to wine appreciation. I was introduced to dinner wines and some excellent white sipping wines in this way.

Some people begin drinking wine because it is much lower in alcohol (10 to 12 percent) than hard liquor, which is 40 to 50 percent alcohol. Because wine mixes well with soda and other soft drinks, it can be a pleasing substitute when you want to limit alcohol consumption.

American magazines and newspapers have also helped introduce people to wine. Wine editors and columnists provide information that sparks interest in wines. In addition, an explosion of wine books has made information available to everyone interested in wine.

In spite of all this—or perhaps because of it—newcomers to wine often do not know where to begin. Two friends of mine, Geraldine and Harold, are good examples.

Geraldine is an elderly, white-haired widow who was given a bottle of white wine for her birthday. That gift from friends served as her introduction to wine; now Geraldine regularly buys and enjoys white wine. She would like to branch out, to serve wine when she entertains her friends, and wants to know what wines to use with foods she enjoys preparing.

Harold is a successful executive who regularly entertains his clients at his favorite restaurants. Wine has always presented a problem for Harold, whose tastes run to whiskey and bourbon. He would like to know how to pronounce the names of wines and to order wines his clients will enjoy. He would even like to begin sampling wines on his own.

This book is for Geraldine and Harold, and for all—beginners or seasoned veterans—who are interested in wine. In it I have shared my own adventure in appreciating wine; as you begin yours, I hope you find it a helpful guide.

To my parents
Rudy and Hazel

Contents

Chapter One

BEGIN AT THE BEGINNING: APPROACHING WINE

Selecting a Wine Store

The most important factor in selecting a wine store may well be the size of the store. Smaller stores usually carry only the largest-selling and most popular brands. Larger stores that specialize in wine can offer the wines of smaller wineries as well. As a rule they have a much larger selection, hence a much greater chance for you to experiment and find some interesting but little-known wines. A larger wine store will also have better storage bins and faster product turnover. As a result, the wine you select will be in its best condition.

Once you have selected a store, find a clerk you like and always do business with that person. Before going to the store, call ahead to see that your clerk is on duty. (I asked my favorite clerk what his hours were, and I do not go to the liquor store except when he is on duty. Now, he even informs me when his hours have changed.) "Your" clerk will soon learn your likes and dislikes and will save some special wines for you to try. Often, when my wine merchant is able to purchase only one case of an excellent wine, he will save four bottles for me and one or two other of his best or favorite customers.

Larger stores also usually have the best bargains. They do a larger volume of business and will often pass their large-lot buying advantage on to their customers. If you are a beginner, however, you may wish to go slowly in your wine purchases. Order single bottles and sample them, following the example of many veteran wine buyers, who at first order single bottles of new or unfamiliar wines. When you find a wine you like, then buy it in case lots. Not only will you have the wine on hand when you need it, but you will be able to take advantage of discounts that are often given on case orders. But don't order more than your storage area can hold; spoiled wine is never a bargain.

Larger wine stores often sponsor wine clubs. A store may give discounts to club members and arrange regular wine tastings. These wine tastings are an inexpensive way to become acquainted with several different wines.

A convenient resource is the Yellow Pages of your telephone book. Look under *Wine—Retail* and make some phone calls. If you are treated well on the phone you will probably get good service in the store. Ask how large the store's wine selection is. If you are aware of four or five wines, ask for them by name. Does the store have them in stock? If not, are they willing to order the wines? How long a wait will you have before your order arrives? Ask for the price of the wines you are interested in, and ask if you can get price breaks for buying several bottles at once. You may be surprised at what you learn through a telephone shopping trip for wine.

The Wine Bottle

When you are at the wine store, your shopping will be more efficient if you know how to "read" the wine bottle. Both the shape and color of a wine bottle are significant. The shape of a bottle is related to the type of wine it contains. (A word of warning; not all wine bottlers follow the "rules," so be sure to read the label.)

The color of the bottle is more important than its shape.

Colored or tinted glass is needed to mask the wine from light. Green has been the traditional color of wine bottles, but recent research has shown brown to be more effective in masking light.

The bottle's color also distinguishes the area from which the wine comes. For instance, Rhine wines (from the Rhine valley) comes in brown bottles and Moselle wines (from the Moselle valley) come in green bottles.

You may wonder about the indentation on the bottom of many bottles, especially those containing sparkling wines. This indentation is the *punt*. It is not there to make the bottle look bigger and thereby reduce the contents. The punt serves a purpose: it helps the sediment settle in the bottle. The sediment is removed, and the bottle is refilled and recorked at the winery before it is shipped to a liquor outlet. A bottle with a punt is actually more expensive to mold than is a flat-bottomed bottle, so, obviously, it is not there to fool you.

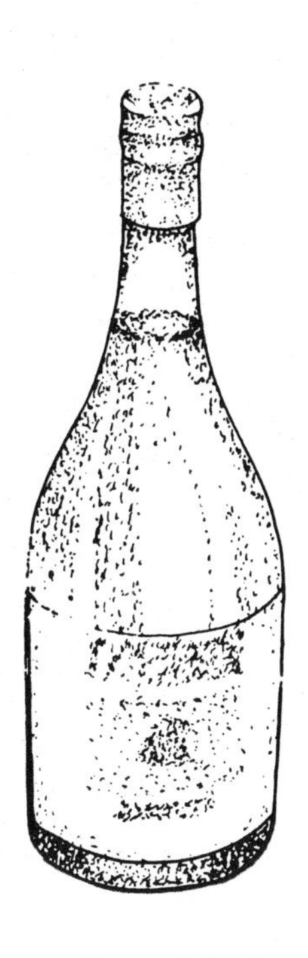

Wines from Many Countries

In the liquor store, you will notice wines from several countries. It is fun and exciting to try wines from all over the world. Such interesting and faraway places as Australia, New Zealand, and Argentina produce wine. The wines of these countries are difficult to find in the United States, but, if they are available in your area, give yourself an oppourtunity to taste them.

The wines of the United States, France, Germany, and Italy, however, are all readily available in the United States. Give them all a place on your table, and continue to buy those you appreciate the most.

French or American: Which Is Best?

For many years, there has been a debate over the comparative qualities of United States and French wines. I have some strong opinions on this subject; I hope you will find my arguments interesting and stimulating. In the past, those in favor of American wines have been on the losing side of this debate, but this has begun to change. I think that California now produces some of the best wines in the world. At the very least, the everyday table wines of California are superior to those of other nations.

There are several reasons for this superiority. First, northern California has a climate that is ideal for winegrowing. Sun, rain and soil combine to make perfect grapes. The counties around San Francisco—Mendocino, Sonoma, Lake, and Napa—provide an ideal setting for grape growing, possibly the finest in the world.

The weather during the year in which the grapes are grown is another important factor in winemaking. Too much rain or too much sun can greatly affect the quality of the year's grapes and, subsequently, the wine. France has three bad years out of every 10, making the date on a bottle of French wine significant. California has never had a bad year; its consistent climate makes the date on a California wine almost meaningless, except in calculating the number of years a wine should be aged before it is drunk. (See *Peak Drinking Age*, Chapter Two.)

In addition to climate, technology has played a vital role in the development of the United States as a premium wine country. It has generally been accepted that Prohibition slowed the development of American winemaking. This is undoubtedly true, but Prohibition also was a blessing in disguise. The interruption in wine production meant that major growth of American vineyards did not begin until after large stainless-steel cooling and fermenting tanks were developed. These tanks allow the winemaker precise control. Fermentation can be stopped at the correct moment by cooling the tank. In more primitive tanks the wine continues to ferment while the bottles are being filled. If it takes three days to bottle or barrel the wine, the last bottles have fermented three days longer than the first, and their quality can differ considerably. Better filtration devices, another improvement in winemaking, have been marketed since the end of World War II. United States vineyards have built from the ground up since the development of these technologies, while French winemakers have remained tied to their older equipment.

Because of their longer growing season, California grapes develop a higher natural sugar content. This means that they are lower in acid than European grapes and that the wine has a generally more pleasing taste. (Some people, however, prefer high-acid wines.) Because aging wine mellows its acidity, and because California grapes are lower in acid to start with, some California wines will reach peak drinking age sooner than European wines.

Sugar content is also related to the alcoholic content of the wine. In general, the higher the sugar content, the higher the percentage of alcohol. However, most nations limit alcoholic content of wines, so this difference is often unimportant.

The higher sugar content of California grapes does not mean that California produces only sweet wines. The length of the fermentation process determines how much of the sugar is converted to alcohol. If fermentation is not stopped until all the sugar has been converted to alcohol, then the wine will be very dry. California produces excellent dry wines.

Wines are aged in barrels before they are bottled, and the wood of the barrel transmits a flavor to the wine. At one time we believed that the differences in flavor between French and California wines were due only to the soil; we now know that the flavor differences can be the result of the different woods used in making the barrels. These flavor differences may not be the result of better or poorer soil.

Snob appeal has played a tremendous role in the debate over French and American wines. French wines have elitist connotations in the minds of many people. If you want to pay extra for snob appeal that is fine, but remember you are not necessarily paying for higher quality. In fact, you may be paying only for a name.

Brandy and Sherry: Wines by Another Name

Many people believe that the great restaurants in the United States were killed by Prohibition because fine wines could no longer be served with the excellent food. Others contend that it was not Prohibition that killed the grand American restaurants, but rather the widespread acceptance of the cocktail during World War I. They believe that drinking hard liquor before dinner deadens the taste buds and that the excellent and subtle flavors of food are lost to palates decimated by the astringency of hard liquor.

If hard liquor dulls the taste buds, what then can we use to prepare our palates for food? The solution to this problem lies in brandy and sherry, members of the wine family. A dry or medium-dry sherry before dinner and a sweet sherry, brandy, or Cognac after dinner make an excellent complement to the dinner itself.

Brandy is made from grapes through a multiple distillation process. Distilling makes brandy different from wine, because wine is not distilled. (Cognac is a brandy that is grown and distilled in the Cognac area of France. To be called Cognac the brandy must be aged at least 15 years. Cognacs receive one star on their label for every five years of age.) California makes some excellent brandies. Always select a brandy that is made by one of the leading vineyards. Winemakers tend to be the best brandy makers because of their familiarity with the grape.

Sherry is a fortified wine. A fortified wine has had additional alcohol added to it; almost always the additional alcohol is in the form of brandy. Wines are usually about 12 percent alcohol, sherries about 20 percent.

We will discuss the several types of sherry in alphabetical order. First is amontillado, a medium-dry sherry that is pale in color and very nice before dinner.

Amoroso is a sweet, dark sherry usually served after dinner. It is similar to the olorosos (sweet, heavy sherries served as dessert).

Cream sherry is any sherry that is sweet. A bottle labeled simply "Cream Sherry" is usually a blend of olorosos.

Fino sherry is any dry sherry. Amontillado is a fino sherry.

Flor, the yeast used in making most dry sherries, is the source of their characteristic taste. Sherries labeled "Flor" have a yeasty taste that most people either like or dislike strongly.

Manzanilla is a pale, dry sherry, a fino. Its salty tang makes it best served before meals.

Oloroso is a sweet, heavy sherry to be served as dessert.

Madeira and Port

Madeira is not a sherry; it is in a class by itself, but we will consider it in this section as it is a member of the grape family. There are four different types of Madeira: Sercial, Rainwater, Bual, and Malmsey. Sercial is the driest type and should be served before dinner. Rainwater is a light Madeira, on the dry side of medium. It should be served before dinner or simply enjoyed by itself. Bual, a sweet Madeira with a taste many people describe as smoky, is an after-dinner or between-meals drink. Malmsey is the sweetest Madeira. It is often described as honey-like or rich.

Port, like Madeira, is not a sherry but it is a grape product. There are two kinds of port: tawny and vintage. Tawny port is aged in wood; vintage port is aged in glass. Both should be taken after dinner.

Vintage: The Date on the Bottle

The vintage—the year the grapes are picked—is usually printed on the wine label. The grapes are picked, crushed, and fermented in the fall of that year. The wine is stored in wood for several months, then bottled in glass and often allowed to rest for several more months before it is released for sale. When you buy the wine, you can choose to drink the bottle immediately if you like young wine. If you like older wines, set the bottle aside to mellow for several months or years. (For further information see *Storing Wines*, later in this chapter, and *Peak Drinking Age* in Chapter Two.)

Some California winemakers do not print a year on their wine labels. Those wines which have no date on the label are called "drink tonight" wines. They are skillfully made to be ready for your table when you bring them home and do not need to be aged. "Drink tonight" wines usually maintain the same high quality from year to year and from bottle to bottle. If you like this wine tonight, you can be sure the next bottle you buy will be the same. Dated wines, on the other hand, usually vary, depending on the year they were produced and the storage conditions they were given. Both vintage and "drink tonight" wines are excellent. One of the pleasures of wines lies in experimenting with both.

How Wines Get Their Names

Wines get their names from three different sources: from grape varieties, from places where the grapes are grown, and from people who handle the wine. Wines named for grape varieties include Pinot noir, Chenin Blanc, Sauvignon Blanc, Zinfandel, Cabernet Sauvignon, Gamay Beaujolais, and many others.

Wines named after the places where they are grown include, among others, Burgundy, Bordeaux, Chablis, Rhine, and Champagne.

Other wines are given names by people involved in the wine business. Vineyard owners, winemakers, producers, bottlers, shippers, and importers have all named wines. Examples of these wines are Le Blanc de Blanc and Chateau La Salle.

Storing Wine

Once you have the wine home from the liquor store you need to store it. It is best to store wine for a month if it has had a long and difficult trip. So give that wine you purchased in Europe a month to recover from its journey. Wouldn't it be nice if you could have that kind of recovery time?

A wine from the neighborhood liquor store needs only two or three days to relax. Wine is a delicate living thing that can be killed by constant vibration. For this reason, it is wise to let wine recover from travel.

All wines should be stored on their sides, to keep the cork moist and insure that it fits snugly against the bottle. If the cork dries out, air will enter the bottle. Wine will deteriorate if it is exposed for very long to air.

The temperature of the storage area should be constant. Find the place in your home where temperature varies the least, like a basement or stairwell. Wide temperature changes will make the wine age too fast. I store wine in an unheated closet, in clay drain tiles that are stacked together. The drain tiles help maintain a lower constant temperature. (To purchase drain tiles, contact your local building materials supplier.) If you wish to invest a great deal of money in wine storage, refrigerated chests that keep a constant temperature of 55 degrees Fahrenheit can be purchased. Do not use old refrigerators because they maintain too low a temperature and do not allow the wine to age.

Store wine in a darkened place. If possible, use a clear (unfrosted) bulb in the area; this type of light will do the least amount of damage. Drain tiles, in addition to keeping temperatures even, provide a dark jacket for the wine.

Wrapping wine in a one-inch thickness of newspaper is another good way to insulate it and keep it cool. The newspaper also provides a dark covering that protects the wine from light.

Store wine with the label up. This makes the label easy to read without moving the bottle more than necessary. In this way, the sediment will always be deposited opposite the label;

this will be helpful if you wish to decant the wine.

Store wines away from appliances with motors or compressors, which vibrate and give off heat. Wines that are vibrated will develop abnormally—they won't like the "bad vibes" they get from nearby appliances.

If you plan on long-term storage of wines, it is especially important for you to follow these rules. Young wines can take abuse much better than older wines; the older the wine is, the more delicately it must be handled.

Storage allows you to have a variety of wines on hand. Wine is an inexpensive treat that you can offer to guests, and it will be available whenever the urge to have wine strikes you.

If wine storage is a problem for you, but if you would still like to buy wines when they are young and inexpensive, then talk with one of your local wine dealers. The dealer may be able to provide you with long-term storage, under excellent conditions, for a nominal charge.

Now that you have purchased the wine and stored it for as long or short a time as you wish, you are ready to serve the wine.

Selecting Wine in a Restaurant

Wine purchased in restaurants is usually more expensive than wine purchased in liquor stores. In fact, wine in restaurants often sells for twice its liquor store price. Because of this, restaurants are a poor place to experiment. If you don't like a wine, it is much more inexpensive to throw it away at home than it is in a restaurant. When in a restaurant, buy only wines you are familiar with.

If nothing on the wine list is familiar to you, ask the wine steward to select a wine for you. Tell him what kind of wines you usually drink and what price range you are willing to pay. He should be capable enough to select a wine that will suit your palate and pocketbook.

If no winemaster is available, and if the person waiting on you seems to have a limited knowledge, then take your chances on a selection of your own or leave the restaurant.

You should always feel free to send back a bottle of wine that is not to your liking. Often in restaurants wine has been improperly stored, or possibly even placed next to a heating vent. Perhaps the wine has just been shipped in that day and has not had adequate time to recover from the jarring it took on its journey to the storeroom. Maybe the wine has been stored standing up rather than lying down and the cork has dried and air has spoiled the wine. You really have no idea how the restaurateur has treated the wine before it came to your table. You have only his reputation to rely on. Simply not liking the wine is also adequate reason to send it back.

When wine is presented to you in a restaurant the person serving it should pour a small amount in your glass so you can taste it and accept or reject the bottle. I always ask that my guest be allowed to have a taste also. Just because you like or dislike a wine does not mean that others at the table will agree with you.

It is a shame that restaurants charge the prices they do for wine. If the price were lower or comparable to liquor store prices the restaurateur would sell more wine and probably make as much profit in the long run. He also would have many more customers who enjoyed their meals and would possibly be willing to return more often. If the restaurateur made a ritual of presenting the wine he would make the meal far more memorable to the customer.

Since restaurateurs are buying their wines wholesale, I think that charging a price equal to the liquor store price plus a modest uncorking fee, say of one dollar, would still allow an adequate profit yet add to the customer's enjoyment.

Since most restaurants do not have large storage areas for wines, most of the wines you receive are young wines. This is fine but you should be aware that the younger reds are harsher than the older, mellower reds you can purchase in liquor stores or age yourself. Sometimes a "drink tonight" red wine is your best purchase in a restaurant. A "drink tonight" wine is one that has no date, no vintage on the label. Paul Masson, Christian Brothers and Gallo make "drink tonight" wines.

In summary:

1. Restaurant wines are usually young.
2. Restaurant wines are generally more expensive than wines purchased in a liquor store.
3. If a winemaster is available use his services.
4. Always feel free to return a wine. No explanation is required; you are the customer.

Many restaurants serve a "house" wine by the glass or by the carafe. These house wines are usually nationally known wines. Ask the service personnel what brand name they serve as a house wine. You may find house wines to be the nicest bargain in the restaurant.

Chapter Two

SERVING WINE

Wine and Food

People who enjoy wine often wonder which wines go with various foods. How are reds, whites, and rosés to be used at the dinner table?

The old axiom, "Red wines with red meat and white wines with white meat," is a valuable rule of thumb. Like all rules, it has exceptions and can be broken by individual tastes. But, like most axioms, this one has lasted because of the truth it contains.

Most white wines have a much more subtle flavor than red wines. White wines go best with meats that also have a subtle flavor—meats like fish, chicken, and veal. The high acidity of white wines serves the same purpose as a lemon wedge served with fish. Both help cut the greasiness of fried fish and the richness of seafood.

Red wines are more robust than white wines. They can overpower the subtle flavors of white meats. Their pronounced flavor goes well with the livelier

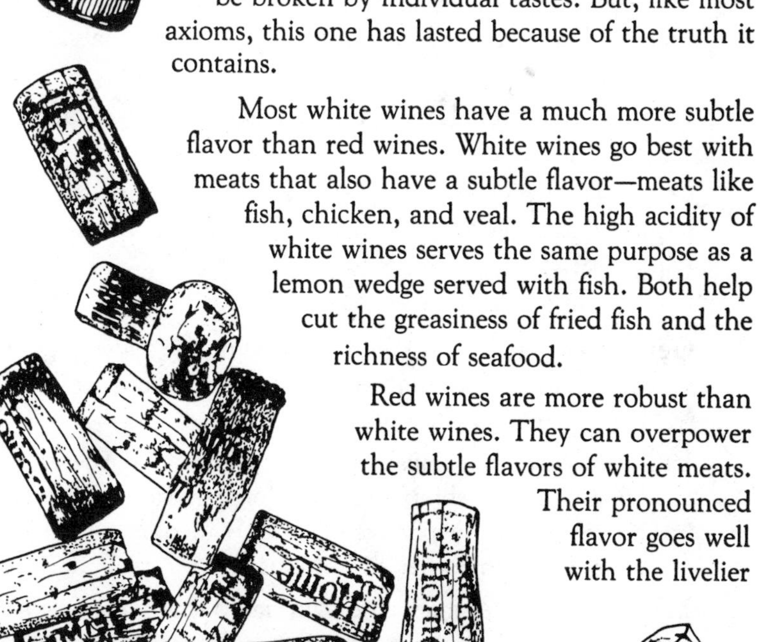

taste of red meats such as beef and lamb.

Rosés can play both sides; many are good with either white or red meats. Try several bottles of rosé and see what you think.

The following list is a simple guide to compatible foods and wines. Appropriate wines are listed for meats and several ethnic cuisines.

Beef—Burgundy, Pinot noir, Bordeaux, Cabernet Sauvignon, Zinfandel; almost all reds.

Chicken—Chardonnay, Pinot Blanc, Riesling, Rhine, Moselle, Chablis, or your favorite white wine.

Corned Beef—With any vinegared or heavily cured meat I recommend serving beer.

Fish—Chardonnay, Pinot Blanc, Riesling, Chablis, Muscadet, Chenin Blanc, Meursault, Graves.

French—For French food, let the meat you are serving be your guide.

Game—Follow the guide for beef. The heavier reds like Cabernet Sauvignon are best.

Game Birds—Light reds are best. Try Pinot noir, Burgundy, or Zinfandel.

German—Germans usually drink wine as a dessert, with cheese and fruit. Try it—it's delicious. Serve beer with German food.

Italian—With red meat serve a Chianti, Barbera, Valpolicella, Nebbiola (Barola), or Bardolino. With white meat serve a Soave or Pinot Bianco. Ask your wine dealer for other suggestions.

Lamb—Serve the same wines with lamb that you serve with beef.

Near Eastern (Greek, Lebanese, Afghan)—With a red meat serve Petit Sirah or Cabernet Sauvignon. With white meat try a Chardonnay or Chenin Blanc. Ask your wine dealer about the flavored

Greek wines such as Retsina.

Pork—See **Chicken.** White wine probably goes best with pork, although many people prefer and recommend a red wine. Try one of the light red wines listed under game birds. Rosé, for many people, is a good compromise for pork, although possibly the best wine to have with pork is a Gewurztraminer. Champagne goes well with ham.

Oriental—Chenin Blanc, Muscat, and Gewurztraminer are excellent with Oriental foods containing white meat. Try a light red with red-meat dishes—those listed with game birds, for example. Beer is excellent with many Oriental foods.

Veal—German wines are especially nice with veal. All wines listed with chicken are also compatible.

Peak Drinking Age

Now that you have selected the meat and the wine you will be serving with your dinner, it is time to check the age of the wine, making sure you are drinking it at its peak. Peak drinking age varies considerably, depending on the variety of grape used and the conditions under which the wine is stored. (Of course, a wine that has no date on the bottle label can be drunk immediately.)

The following chart is a list of approximate ages at which wines should be consumed. If your wine has a place name, use the place-name chart to determine the grape variety.

Wine	Peak Drinking Age
Cabernet Sauvignon	8-15 years
Chenin Blanc	2- 5 years
Gamay Beaujolais	3- 5 years
Pinot Blanc	4 years
Pinot Chardonnay	2- 5 years
Pinot noir	3- 6 years
Sauvignon Blanc	2- 5 years
Semillon	2- 5 years
Sylvander	3 years
Reisling	3 years
Zinfandel	5- 8 years

Place-Name Wines	Grape Variety
Beaujolais	Gamay Beaujolais
Bordeaux	Cabernet Sauvignon
Burgundy	Pinot noir and Gamay Beaujolais
Chablis	Chenin Blanc, Pinot Chardonnay
Champagne	Pinot noir (with many exceptions)
Claret	Cabernet Sauvignon
Graves	Semillon and Sauvignon Blanc
Loire	Muscadet, Chenin Blanc, Chasselas
Medoc	Cabernet Sauvignon
Moselle	Riesling
Pouilly - Fuisse	Pinot Chardonnay
Pouilly - Fume	Sauvignon Blanc
Rhine	Sylvander and Reisling
Sauterne	Sauvignon Blanc and Semillon
Vouvray	Chenin Blanc
White Burgundy	Pinot Blanc

This chart can be used if your wine store is out of your favorite type of wine. For instance, if you like a Burgundy but none is available, a Pinot noir would be a good substitute.

Temperature

When you have selected your food and your wine and found the wine's prime drinking age, it is time to determine the best serving temperature for the wine.

Most reds should be served slightly below room temperature, at about 60 to 65 degrees Fahrenheit. For this reason, it is best to store red wines in the coolest part of your house; at cool room temperature, red wines develop their maximum flavor, bouquet, and aroma. Red wines are very heavy. If they are stored and served at a temperature that is too low, the molecules in the wine will have trouble breaking the surface. The warmer the liquid, the easier it is for the molecules to break the surface tension, escape, and give off the aroma and bouquet that make red wine so enjoyable. Exceptions to this temperature rule are Lambrusco and Cold Duck. Both should be served cold, at about 40 degrees Fahrenheit (two hours in a refrigerator or one hour in an ice bucket).

White and rosé wines are almost always served chilled, at about 50 to 55 degrees Fahrenheit. The molecular structure of white wine is light, and the molecules must be prevented from escaping in order to preserve the wine's flavor and scent. Many people like their white wines served even colder, at about 40 degrees. White wine that cold may lose a great deal of its character. Experiment and serve it the way you like it.

Champagne—white, pink or red—should be served cold, at about 40 degrees Fahrenheit.

Some general rules for serving wine: Always follow the instructions on the label, if any are given. Room temperature means about 60 to 65 degrees Fahrenheit, chilled means about 50 to 55 degrees Fahrenheit, and cold means about 40 degrees Fahrenheit. An ice bucket should be used only for Champagne, or for Lambrusco or Cold Duck. (An ice bucket should never be used for any other red wines.) Ice will keep white wines too cold, although I like to set my white wine bottle in an ice bucket with a layer of ice in the bottom. This helps the white wine maintain its chill.

Corkscrews

The food is prepared, the wine is ready; now it is time to open the bottle.

Four types of corkscrews—the jackknife, the wing type, the needle or air type, and the double-prong type—are commonly used. The jackknife corkscrew (see illustration) is used by most professionals. The knife (A) is used to remove the foil covering the cork. Some wine bottles have a plastic cap over the cork; the knife works well for removing this also. The corkscrew (B) is inserted into the cork. The entire device is turned, forcing the screw into the cork. The hook (C) is placed over the bottle lip to extract the cork. By pushing up at D the cork is forced from the neck of the bottle. This corkscrew is the best type on the market and I recommend it highly. Its major drawback is that it requires some muscle to extract the cork.

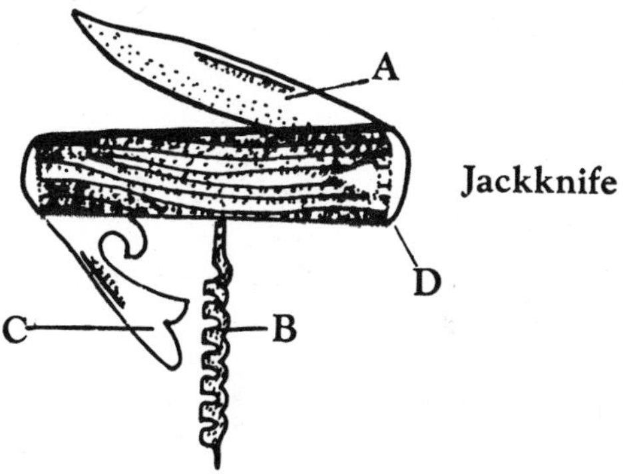

Jackknife

A second type, the wing corkscrew, is efficient and easy to operate. By looking at the illustration you will get a good idea of how this corkscrew works. Insert the corkscrew (A) into the cork until the device is snug against the top of the bottle

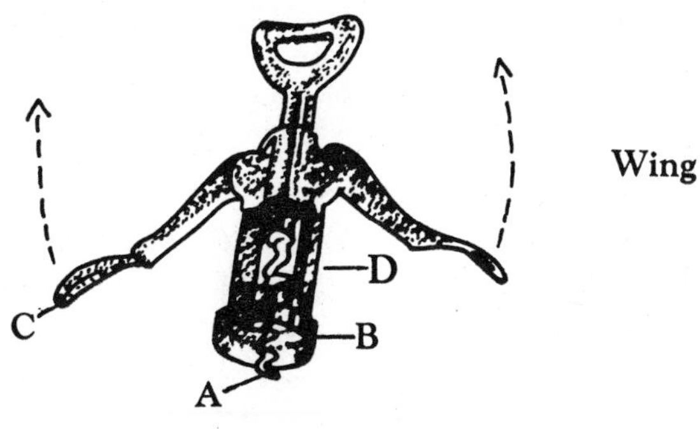

Wing

(B). As the corkscrew is inserted the wings or arms (C) will rise. To remove the cork, simply press down on the wings; the cork will be pulled up into the body (D) of the device. If you purchase a wing-type corkscrew be sure to get one with a curly-cue (open) screw; otherwise you will not get a good grip on the cork and it will be difficult to extract from the bottle.

Needle or Air

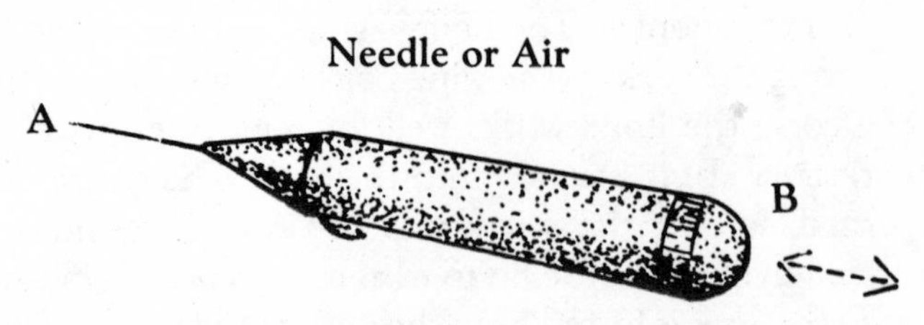

The needle or air-type corkscrew arouses a lot of curiosity. To operate this corkscrew, you insert the needle (A) into the cork. Make sure the needle is pushed all the way through the cork. You then pump air into the bottle (B), forcing the cork up and out. Warning! This corkscrew must be used only on bottles of traditional shape. It can be dangerous if used on odd-shaped bottles; the bottle will explode, sending little glass missiles throughout the room.

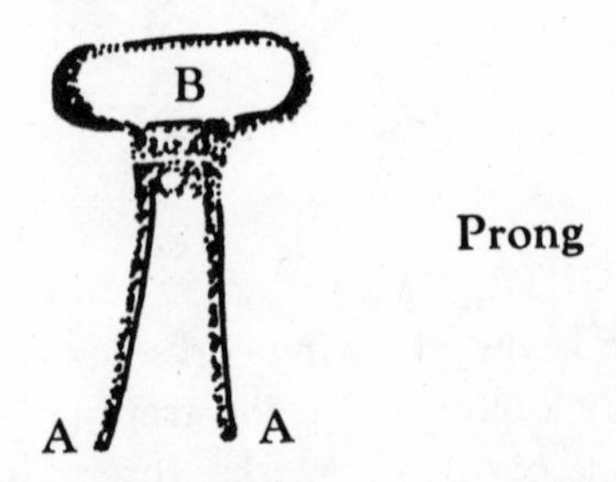

Prong

The prong-type corkscrew is quite a conversation piece. Two prongs (A) are inserted between the cork and the bottle until the handle (B) is snug against the bottle lip. Simply pull up the handle and remove the cork. This corkscrew takes some patience; inserting the prongs can be a time-consuming job. The major advantage of this corkscrew is that you can extract the cork without doing damage to it. This means that the cork can be reused and that no pieces of cork can splinter off into the wine.

Uncorking Champagne requires no corkscrew. Simply remove the wire cap and, placing your palm over the cork, turn and twist gently until it is removed. Many people like to place a napkin over the cork in case it gets away from them; the cork will then be caught in the napkin and will not fly into the room, possibly injuring someone or breaking an object. There is a tremendous amount of pressure in a Champagne bottle; that pressure must be respected.

Examining the Cork

After extracting the cork, look for wine stains along its side. Stains that run the length of the cork could be a bad sign; this means air has entered the bottle and possibly destroyed the wine.

Now smell the end of the cork that was in the bottle. If it smells like vinegar the wine is almost certainly bad.

Pass the cork around for guests to examine. I will never forget the time I presented a red-wine cork to the young daughter of one of my guests. I asked her how it smelled and she replied that it smelled like cork.

Breathing

Breathing means allowing red wine to be exposed to the air before serving. This increases and mellows the flavor of the wine.

When we speak of breathing wines we are always talking about red wines. Both the youngest and the heaviest of the reds should be opened at least one and one-half hours before serving. Older and/or lighter reds should be opened about one-half hour before serving. Very old red wines are opened and drunk immediately. Many older wines are good for just a few minutes; they deteriorate rapidly when exposed to air.

If you do not decant your red wines (see next section), then pour a small amount of the wine into a glass so the top of the wine in the bottle is below the neck. A greater surface area of the wine will then be exposed to the air.

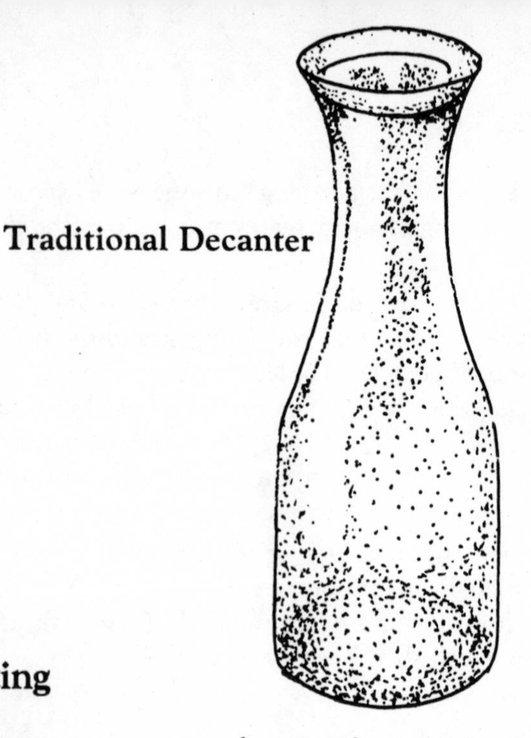
Traditional Decanter

Decanting

Decanting means pouring the wine from the bottle into another container. The new container can be simple or ornate. Decanters for red wines have wide-mouth openings; they do not have covers or stoppers. Narrow-neck decanters with stoppers are intended for port and sherry.

Decanting has a twofold purpose. It aerates the wine—that is, it exposes it to air. This enlivens the flavor of the wine. Decanting also removes sediment; however, usually only old wines have sediment.

Even though decanting is unnecessary except for the older wines, it is fun and can be done for the sheer pleasure of impressing guests and adding to the ritual of eating and drinking.

Decanting is a very simple procedure. Set the bottle upright overnight so any sediment will settle to the bottom. Uncork the wine. Pour it, label up, in a fine, steady stream into the decanter. Watch the stream closely. As soon as you see sediment stop pouring. Some people recommend that you hold a candle, lightbulb, or flashlight under the neck of the bottle to aid you in seeing the sediment. If pouring during the day, you can use sunlight from a window to help you see the sediment.

Wine Glasses

There are several different types of wine glasses. Each is designed to provide the best service for the type of wine to be served.

Using the appropriate glasses for various wines adds to the enjoyment of wine. One of the many pleasures in wine drinking is found in following the rituals. They are not just for snobs; they have a purpose.

Bordeaux

The Bordeaux glass is shaped to direct the scent of the heavier red wines to the nose. It is intended to be used with Bordeaux, Claret, and Cabernet Sauvignon wines. Its size is usually about 10 ounces. An 8-to 10-ounce glass in this shape makes an excellent all-purpose wine glass that can be used to serve all reds and sherries. Your collection of glassware can be expanded after making an initial investment in this style of glass.

Burgundy

Burgundy glasses are designed to be used with light red wines like Burgundy, Pinot noir, and Zinfandel. The Burgundy glass is about 12 to 14 ounces in size.

White

The white-wine glass is the same shape as the Bordeaux glass; it simply has shorter sides. The scent of white wines is released more easily than the scent of reds and does not need to be directed as much toward your nose. This glass is generally about six ounces in size.

German White

The German white-wine glass, traditionally used to serve German wines, has a longer stem than does the regular white-wine glass. It holds about nine ounces.

Tulip and Fluted (Trumpeted) Champagne

Champagne glasses come in several shapes. The best and most highly recommended are the tulip and fluted or trumpeted glasses. Both of these glasses are tall and nicely display the constantly rising bubbles that are characteristic of Champagne.

Hollow-stemmed Champagne

The hollow-stemmed Champagne glass also provides a view of rising bubbles, but it is not nearly as dramatic as either the tulip or fluted glasses. Other glasses are shaped like hollow-stemmed glasses but do not have the hollow stem. They are absolutely worthless as Champagne glasses. These shallow, wide glasses, commonly used in the United States, should all be broken and replaced with the far more interesting tulip or fluted glasses.

Brandy Snifter

The brandy or Cognac snifter is designed to be cupped in the hand. This allows the hand to warm and swirl the brandy. The snifter glass comes in many different sizes, from a small two-ounce capacity to a giant 20-ounce monster. The best size for practical use is about eight ounces.

Sherry or Port

The best glasses to use for sherry and port are the same shape as the Bordeaux glass except they are smaller, running about five ounces.

Many people prefer glassware with a narrow rim over glasses with a slight enlargement at the rim. They insist the narrow rim feels better on their lips. It is also a sign of better glassware.

An inexpensive set of glassware can serve you well for years; it will also be dishwasher-safe. Expensive glassware has a pleasant and delicate feel but is more easily breakable and often must be washed by hand.

Presenting the Wine

You are now ready to bring the wine to the table. To present the wine, the host should pour a swallow into his glass, swirl the wine, sniff it, and drink it. If the wine is good, he can then pour it for his guests. It may seem inappropriate for the host to drink first, but in this way a guest will not taste wine that may have gone bad. Also, any pieces of cork in the wine will fall into the host's glass.

Always pour wine from the guest's right-hand side. At informal occasions, simply pass the bottle.

Red- and white-wine glasses should be filled only about one-third full so that the wine can be swirled and sniffed. Filling a glass too full prevents it from serving its function—directing the wine's scent to the nose of the drinker. Champagne glasses should be filled so you can see the rising bubbles. A brandy snifter should have only one or two ounces poured into it so that the brandy can be easily warmed.

Some people like to cover the wine bottle with a white towel. This helps hold the cellar temperature or the chill. Other people feel it is incorrect to cover a wine bottle, that their guests have a right to see what they are drinking. A suggestion: show your guests the bottle, then wrap it.

If you are having more than one wine at your dinner or party, you should start the evening with a dry wine and progress to sweeter wines.

Holding the Glass

There are some sensible rules about holding the wine glass.

The wine glass should always be picked up by the stem. If you pick it up by the bowl you will leave fingerprints, which will make it difficult to see through the glass and to check on the wine's appearance.

Holding the glass at the stem also keeps your hand further away from your nose. This is important because the soap and perfume scents from your hands can interfere with the aroma and bouquet of the wine. Also, if you hold the bowl of the glass, the warmth of your hand will heat up the wine, and it will not retain its best temperature.

Swirling the wine in the glass helps release the wine's subtle flavor by breaking the surface tension and by coating the glass with a thin layer of wine.

You will notice that after swirling the wine, droplets begin to form at the top of the swirl. As the droplets gather together, they start to run down the side of the wine glass. These streams are called legs, and they are caused by the presence of glycerin in the wine. In the past legs were a sign of quality. Now, however, it is a simple matter for winemakers to add glycerin to wine and cause the legs to form on the glass. Do not be misled by legs.

Washing Your Wine Glasses

If you have inexpensive and sturdy glassware, you should wash it in your automatic dishwasher, a great convenience. But expensive, more delicate crystal glassware will have to be washed by hand. An automatic dishwasher would be too rough and would probably break the glasses or scar their surfaces.

Begin washing by dipping and swirling a single glass in hot, sudsy water. Then dip the glass in hot, clear water to remove the suds and set it aside to drain. If you wish to wipe the glasses, use a lint-free cloth. You are now ready to store your glassware.

Storing Your Wine Glasses

Always store wine glasses with the bowl down. This prevents dust from settling inside the bowl and causing a bad taste the next time you serve wine.

If you do not use your wine glasses often, heaven forbid, the air trapped inside the inverted bowl will get musty. This can affect the flavor of the wine. To prevent mustiness, store the glasses on a rough surface so that air can circulate through the bowl. A shelf liner of corrugated cardboard makes for excellent circulation.

Many people prefer to hang their wine glasses to avoid mustiness in the bowl. Hanging glasses are very decorative, but be careful—one swinging glass can lead to two broken glasses.

Cleaning Your Wine Decanter

If you decant sherry or port you will notice as time passes that a stain begins to form inside the decanter. How do you remove these stains? The best and least expensive method is to fill the decanter with clean sand, add enough water to moisten the sand, and shake the decanter. The abrasive action of the sand will remove the stain. This may take a while, but it is an effective procedure, and it will not leave any chemical residue that can sour the taste of your sherry or port.

Removing Labels

You may want to collect labels from wines you have drunk. A quick hot-water bath is the most effective method of safely removing labels. Hold the bottle by the neck, over a stopped sink, and pour boiling water from a tea kettle over the label. After several seconds the label should loosen and fall into the sink. If the label is stubborn, place the bottle in the water so that the label can soak for a few minutes, then gently loosen it. To dry the label, place it between two sheets of paper towel and pat dry.

Wine journals are available for storing labels, but I prefer pasting them on the back of 5-by-8-inch cards on which I have made comments about the wines. The cards can be easily alphabetized in a recipe box. (See Chapter Three.)

Wine Equipment

The Cork Fisher

The cork fisher is a very small spoon with a hole in the bowl. It is used to fish out any cork pieces that may have fallen into the bottle during uncorking.

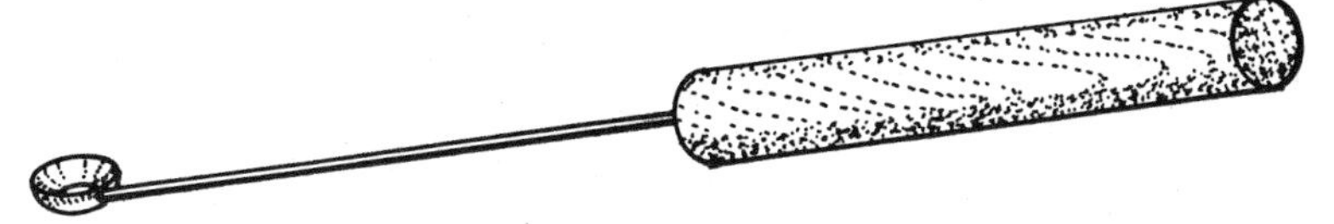

The Tastevin

The tastevin is used by winemakers, in restaurants, and in vineyards.

The chain is placed around the neck. The shallow bowl, with a glass bottom, is filled with wine. The glass bottom allows the clarity of the wine to be checked by holding the tastevin over a lighted candle. The wine can also be tasted from the tastevin.

Tastevins are usually made of silver and are most commonly used in the Burgundy area of France.

The Wine Funnel

The wine funnel is made of glass and can be used to decant the wine. Some decanters have very small necks and the funnel makes the pouring of the wine to a second container much easier because of its wide mouth. It serves basically the same purpose as any funnel. The glass allows you to view the wine as it is being decanted so you can check the clarity.

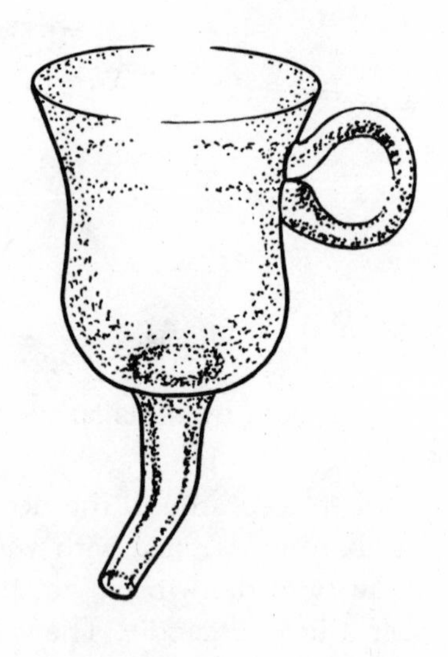

Chapter Three

TASTING AND RATING WINE

How to Drink Wine

There is much more to drinking wine than lifting a glass to your mouth and swallowing. This chapter will help you learn to taste and compare wines so that you can develop your own rating system.

The human tongue can discern only four properties: saltiness, sweetness, sourness, and bitterness. Wine has more than 150 properties; obviously, to really enjoy wine you must do more than just swallow it. In order to get the full essence of wine it is necessary to use the nose, which can detect more than 4,000 properties.

But sniffing wine is a gentle art that must be approached with caution. Long deep breaths will cause the nasal passages to become overstimulated and lose their ability to help you get the most from your wine. Your nose will become insensitive to the fine nuances of wine.

The correct way to sniff and swallow wine begins with swirling the wine in the glass a couple of times. This helps release the wine's aroma and bouquet. Inhale some of the aroma into the lungs and hold it there. Take a drink of the wine and rotate it in the mouth so that it covers your entire palate. (This, of course, should be done in a socially acceptable manner with a minimum of cheek movement and mouth noises.) Swallow most of the wine. Breathe out through the nose, expelling the warmed vapor from your lungs. Swallow the rest of the wine. You will notice a slight feeling of lightheadedness after swallowing. The entire back of your nose and throat will taste the wine, and you will be surprised at how much more you are enjoying it.

Does the process of sniffing and swallowing wine sound like a lot of bother? Actually, it takes only a few seconds to accomplish. With a little practice, it will become a habit and you will do it without giving the process the slightest thought. And it will certainly add to your enjoyment and appreciation of wine.

The James Bond Fallacy

Have you ever seen a James Bond movie? In those films, Agent 007 is a wizard of wine. He can tell not only the year a wine's grapes were picked, but the month and the day of the picking as well. He can identify the type of wine he is drinking; after one sip he can tell whether it is a Beaujolais or a Burgundy. Mr. Bond can identify the grower, the cuvee (batch) number and soil type, and tell how long the wine was aged in wood before it was bottled.

Almost everyone would like to have the knowledge of wine that the great agent of Ian Fleming's imagination does. Unfortunately, James Bond's amazing feats are possible only in imagination. The best winetasters in the world cannot give the kinds of information about wine that 007 dispenses so confidently.

What *can* a winetaster tell you?

An expert winetaster, when presented with two wines poured into three glasses each, can identify which glasses contain the same wine. A superior winetaster might be able to identify the kind of wine being tasted, but even that is unlikely. He would not be able to tell you the brand name of the wine or the year or soil type in which the grapes were grown. In other words, an expert winetaster does not accomplish the superhuman feats of Agent 007. An expert winetaster has no skills you cannot develop yourself. Don't be intimidated by the stupendous accomplishments of fictional heroes. You can be a winetaster; you can tell what you like to drink. *You* are capable of great tastings.

You Are the Winetaster:

Tasting, Rating, and Recording Information About Wines

It is very satisfying to taste and rate wine on your own. By keeping records you will be able to refer back to wines you liked; you can purchase by name wines that you had at a friend's home or in a restaurant. Wines you enjoyed months ago need not be forgotten, because you can have a way of identifying wines you appreciated and avoiding those you did not like.

This section includes a guide to taking notes on wines that you drink. The guide is similar to a note-taking system used by professional winetasters. I have changed the names of some of the qualities being rated and have made changes in the point totals accorded some elements. Greater point totals have been given to those qualities that are more easily measured than others.

In this system, wine is judged by assessing five characteristics. Each characteristic is assigned a number of possible points. An overall total of 20 points is possible.

Category	Number of Points Possible
Appearance	4
Scent	4
Taste	6
Body	3
Finish	3
Total	20

After you have rated the wine for each category and added up the total points, the wine can be judged from poor to excellent by the total number of points you assign it. Use the following table as a guide.

Total Points	Rating
0 - 12	poor
13 - 14	fair
15 - 17	good
18 - 20	excellent

On the following page is a facsimile of the Andersen Wine Tasting Note Card. The spaces for recording rating points, specific comments, and general comments are intended to help you remember what the wine was like. The wine-name and brand-name sections are necessary if you intend to order more of the wine. The difference between the vintage date and the tasting date will tell you the age of the wine when you tasted it.

How do we rate a wine? Let us take a detailed look at each of the sections on the Andersen Wine Tasting Note Card.

The Andersen Wine Tasting Note Card

Wine Name:

RATING POINTS			COMMENTS
Appearance	4	______	______________________
Scent	4	______	______________________
Taste	6	______	______________________
Body	3	______	______________________
Finish	3	______	______________________
Total	20	______	______________________

Brand Name: ______________________ Price: __________

Tasting Date: ______________ Vintage Date: ______________

General Comments: ______________________

____

____

The Andersen Wine Tasting Note Card

Wine Name:

RATING POINTS			COMMENTS
Appearance	4	______	______________________
Scent	4	______	______________________
Taste	6	______	______________________
Body	3	______	______________________
Finish	3	______	______________________
Total	20	______	______________________

Brand Name: ______________________ Price: __________

Tasting Date: ______________________ Vintage Date: __________

General Comments: ______________________

The Andersen Wine Tasting Note Card

Wine Name:

RATING POINTS			COMMENTS
Appearance	4	________	______________________
Scent	4	________	______________________
Taste	6	________	______________________
Body	3	________	______________________
Finish	3	________	______________________
Total	20	________	______________________

Brand Name: ______________________ Price: __________

Tasting Date: ______________ Vintage Date: ______________

General Comments: ______________________

____

____

APPEARANCE—4 points
Color—2 points

Age	Red Wine	White Wine	Rosé Wine
Young	Purple	Green (clear)	Pink
Medium-aged	Red	Yellow	Light Red
Old	Brown	Gold	Orange

The older a wine, the darker its color will be. Check the wine to see if the age matches the prescribed color. Does the wine have a color other than the one it should? Subtract points for variations in color.

Transparency—2 points

Bright
Clear
Hazy
Cloudy

A cloudy look is usually a bad sign in wine. Sediment, on the other hand, is not necessarily a bad sign. Sediment can be an indication that the wine is older or that it has suffered from poor decanting or improper handling. Do not degrade the wine for sediment. A cloudy or hazy appearance, however, should result in loss of points.

SCENT—4 points
Bouquet—2 points

The bouquet of a wine is the smell of the grape in the wine. Is the smell of the grape pleasant and mild or harsh and bitter?

Does the wine smell like the grape variety from which it is made? Experience at tasting a particular grape variety will tell you if the wine smells as it should. A pronounced smell of the grape is said to give the wine a "foxy" smell. If the wine has only a very slight smell of the grape we say that it is "soft."

Does the wine have the smell of its traditional place name?

Again, your ability to discern this will increase with experience. Start keeping records. Occasionally go through your notes to reinforce your knowledge of what the wines smelled and tasted like to you.

Aroma—2 points

The aroma of a wine is any scent in the wine of the fermentation process.

Is a yeasty or moldy smell present? This is not necessarily a negative quality. Many people enjoy the smell and taste of yeast or mold, which are the results of the fermentation process. If you enjoy those aspects of a wine rate the wine high.

Most sherries are on the yeasty side, and one, flor sherry, should have a dominant yeasty smell and taste.

Are there any "off" odors in the wine? If anything about the wine smells unpleasant or unfamiliar for that type of wine then deduct points as this is a negative feature.

It is difficult to define and describe the aroma and bouquet of many wines. However, wine experts have noticed pronounced scents in several wine varieties. Some place-name wines also have distinct scents. The following chart may be helpful in determining if a wine is within its normal range of aroma and bouquet.

Wine Name	Scent
Burgundy	earthy
Chablis	metallic or steely
Cabernet Sauvignon	herby, green olive, currants, cedar
Chardonnay	fruity, smokey, apple
Chenin Blanc	flinty, steely, metallic
Moselle	flowery
Pinot noir	peppermint
Reisling	flowery, fruity, honey, tart

Rhine	fruity, raw apple
Sauvignon Blanc	spicey, fruity, olive
Zinfandel	raspberries

TASTE—6 points
Dry-Sweet Scale—2 points

Brut (extra dry)
Dry (very dry)
Sec (medium)
Sweet

The drier a wine, the less sugar it contains. Dry wines have a great deal of pucker power. The longer a wine is allowed to ferment, the greater the amount of sugar in the grape is converted to alcohol and the drier the wine will be. Sometimes additional sugar is added to wine to make it even sweeter than the grape's natural sugar content would allow.

Preferences for dryness and sweetness are a matter of personal choice. Whether you choose a dry or white wine also depends on the foods with which the wine may be served. Dry wines are best with before-dinner snacks, soups, and entrees. Medium wines often go well with soup and entrees. Sweet wines are an excellent complement to desserts. Personal palate and compatibility with foods that match the wine's characteristics are a good measure for granting or deducting points in this section.

Flavor—4 points

Flavor, like aroma and bouquet, can be difficult to judge without some experience behind you. As you taste wines and record your findings, you will soon build up a backlog of experience. You will be able to compare new tastings with old tastings. The most important question is, "Does the wine taste like the grape variety from which it is made?" Take another look at the section on scent. Wines should generally taste the way they smell. Compare the taste with the characteristic scents listed on the chart in the scent section. Be certain to notice and record any exceptional or "off" tastes.

BODY—3 points

Body is a difficult aspect of wine to define and measure. Body is generally thought to be, in large part, the alcoholic content of the wine. But alcoholic content is usually set by law in both the country of origin and the importing country. Since most wines have approximately the same alcoholic content, it is meaningless to measure body by this standard. Do not judge body simply by looking at the alcoholic percentage listed on the wine bottle label.

What then is a good measure of body? The feel of the wine on your tongue and in your mouth is probably the best guide. Does the wine, when measured against the feel characteristic of its variety, seem light or heavy on the tongue? Does it seem "full" or is it watery?

Be certain to compare only wines of the same type against one another. A Pinot noir should feel lighter than a Cabernet Sauvignon. White wines should be lighter than red wines.

FINISH—3 points

Finish is the length of the aftertaste of the wine, and it is a reliable measure of the wine's quality. A long aftertaste is a sign of excellence. Too much is too much, of course, but wine with little or no aftertaste is a disappointment.

COMMENTS

In the space reserved for comments, on the right side of the Andersen Wine Tasting Note Card, you can write remarks and answer the questions for each of the five qualities of the wine. This will give you a clearer indication of what each wine is like than if you simply granted points. Comments are very helpful when you review your wine cards in the future.

GENERAL COMMENTS

Under general comments, at the bottom left of the note card, you may wish to indicate how the wine was used. Was it drunk with a meal, as a dessert, before dinner, or simply by itself? What kind of food accompanied the wine? If you had guests, who were they? Indicate how the wine went with the occasion or food served. Make suggestions as to how it might better be used in the future. Indicate whether or not you would like to buy this wine again.

You are now ready to judge wines. You know the elements of wine appreciation. It is now time to become familiar with some of the terms used in describing wines. These terms will help you make intelligent, well defined comments about wine.

Wine Tasting Terms

The following list will acquaint you with some of the basic terms dealing with the many qualities of wines. Many of the terms should be used with descriptive adjectives like excellent, superior, fair, good, or bad. The list is short enough to allow you to page through it as you are tasting wines. You will soon become familiar with the terms and will find yourself using them in conversations about wine.

Balance. A wine that tastes as it should is well balanced. No one aspect of the wine masks any other aspect. A well balanced wine has no single element dominating over its other elements.

Big. A big wine has a great deal of flavor, body, and scent.

Bitter. One of the four tastes the tongue can detect. It is generally a part of the aftertaste and should not be considered a negative quality. Many people enjoy a wine with a bitter taste.

Body. The feel of the wine in the mouth. Body can be described as coarse, heavy, full, or delicate. Each of these four terms is defined in this glossary. Use them when describing body in the comments section of the Andersen Wine Tasting Note Card.

Character. The qualities of a particular grape that should always be present in the wine of that grape variety. If any peculiar grape tastes are present in the wine we would say that the wine has bad character.

Clean. A wine that is clean has no strange tastes. A clean wine is very pleasing to the palate.

Cloudy. A cloudy wine has a foggy appearance that is unpleasant to the eye. A bad sign.

Coarse. A wine that is too heavy is said to be coarse. A coarse wine has too much body, too heavy a feel in the mouth. The body of the wine masks the other properties the wine should have. Heavy, full, and delicate are other terms used to describe the body of wine. All three of these terms are defined in this glossary.

Common. A term used in ranking wines. (See *Ranking.*)

Corky. If the flavor of the cork has been transmitted to the wine we say that the wine is corky.

Delicate. A delicate wine has a very light taste and feel in the mouth. (See *Body.*)

Distinguished. The highest ranking a wine can receive. A superior wine. (See *Ranking.*)

Dry. A dry wine has had most or all of its sugar converted to alcohol. Dry can be said to be the opposite of sweet. A dry wine has a great deal of pucker power in the mouth.

Dull. A dull wine is uninteresting—and probably undrinkable. Dull is a term used in ranking wines. (See *Ranking.*)

Earthy. An earthy wine is one that has a taste of soil. Earthiness is not a bad quality in wine; it is sought in some wines.

Elegant. A good, but not distinguished, wine. Elegant is a term used in ranking wines. (See *Ranking.*)

Fat. Fat has the same meaning as big. (See *Big.*)

Fine. Better than elegant, less than distinguished. (See *Ranking.*)

Flinty. A term most often used to describe white wines. Chablis should have this quality. Flintiness is a steely or metallic taste in a wine.

Flowery. A term applied to the bouquet of many white wines. A Moselle wine should have this scent.

Foxy. A foxy wine has a heavy and pronounced grape taste. Lambrusco and kosher wines are foxy. A foxy taste might mean that a wine is poorly balanced, but foxiness is not necessarily a negative quality. A great many people enjoy foxy wines.

Fragrant. If a wine has a pronounced scent or smell we say that it is fragrant.

Fresh. A wine is said to be fresh if it has a cool, crisp taste. The taste of a very young wine is often described as fresh.

Fruity. A wine that tastes and smells like fruit is said to be fruity. A Zinfandel should smell like raspberries. White wines often taste somewhat like raw apple.

Full. Fullness is an aspect of body. (See *Body.*) A full-bodied wine is a wine with a light but easily discernable taste.

Grapey. See *Foxy.*

Green. A harsh, raw, vinegary taste, generally found in a white wine. The term can also be used to describe young red wines.

Hard. A wine that needs to be mellowed is said to be hard. Often young wines are said to be hard or harsh.

Heavy. A term used to describe the body of wine. (See *Body.*) A heavy wine has a pronounced, not a delicate, taste.

Metallic. See *Flinty.*

Moldy. A moldy wine has the taste and smell of mold. In a red wine, this is considered unpleasant. It is caused by the use of moldy grapes in the winemaking. Some white wines are deliberately made from moldy grapes and should have this characteristic scent and smell.

Musty. Wine that has been stored in unclean casks and cellars has an unpleasant taste and smell referred to as musty. A musty taste can also be caused by improper storage of the glassware from which you are drinking. In any case, it is definitely a negative characteristic. (See *Storing Your Wine Glasses* and *Washing Your Wine Glasses*, Chapter Two.)

Nose. Any wine with a pronounced scent is said to have a lot of nose. A wine with little aroma and bouquet has a light nose.

Nutty. A term used to describe the taste of many sherries. You have not lived until you have eaten raw walnuts with sherry.

Oaky. See *Woody.*

Off. When a wine has an off taste it does not taste as it should.

Poor. A very low-quality wine. (See *Ranking.*)

Powerful. A wine that has a pronounced flavor and scent is described as powerful.

Ranking. Six terms, listed here from highest to lowest, are used to rank wines: distinguished, fine, elegant, common, poor, and dull.

Ripe. Ripe is often used to describe a white, semi-sweet, fruity, mellow wine. It is also used to describe a wine that is ready to drink, one that needs no further aging.

Robe. Often used to describe a wine's appearance—its color and transparency. (A further definition of appearance can be found in *You Are the Winetaster: Tasting, Rating and Recording Information about Wines,* earlier in this chapter.) A cloudy, off-color wine is said to have a bad robe.

Robust. A full-bodied, slightly harsh red wine is said to be robust. This term has always seemed to me to be a combination of the terms *big* and *green.*

Rounded. A wine with no shortcomings would be called rounded.

Silky. An unusually smooth wine.

Small. A term applied to ordinary wines. Small is not a negative term, it simply means not grand. It is equivalent to common on the rating scale.

Smooth. A silky, velvety feel.

Soapy. Dull, flat, low-acid, disagreeable.

Soft. A soft wine is not harsh. It has no pronounced flavor or aftertaste.

Sound. A sound wine has no defects.

Sour. A wine that is turning or has turned to vinegar is said to be sour. A sour wine cannot be drunk.

Spicy. A spicy wine is one with the flavor or scent of spices. Gewutztraminer is a German wine whose name means spicy wine.

Steely. See *Flinty.*

Stemmy. A bitter, woody, fibrous taste acquired by wines that are fermented with the grape stems. A negative characteristic.

Sweet. A wine with a sugary taste. Sweet wines can range from Monbazillac and sweet Sauterne, which are syrupy, to wines with a very light touch of sweetness, such as many Chenin Blancs. Dry is the opposite of sweet in wine terminology.

Tart. A wine that is high in acid is tart. Most white wines and many young reds are tart.

Tender. A young wine.

Thin. A watery, low-alcohol wine is thin.

Velvety. A velvety wine is one that has a soft, silky, smooth feel. (See *Soft*, *Silky*, and *Smooth.*)

Watery. See *Thin.*

Woody. The taste of wood in the wine. Many people enjoy a slight woody taste. However, if wine is left in the barrel too long it can acquire a negative woody taste. Do not confuse woodiness and stemminess; they are two quite different qualities.

Chapter Four

A HISTORY OF WINE

Wine has played an important role as food in the history of man. Grape seeds have been found at archaeological sites that date from prehistoric times and the early Egyptians left excellent records, cut in stone, of their winemaking techniques.

The Fertile Crescent extending from the Tigris-Euphrates River Valley to the Holy Lands area was the scene of winemaking at an early date. The Code of Hammurabi, an early book of laws from the Fertile Crescent, prohibits the diluting of wine with water. The Code was written in the 18th century B.C.

In the ancient world wine was one of a handful of foods that could be preserved.

Covered pots and underground storage vats indicate that men realized early the harmful effects of air on wine.

The ancient Greeks had vineyards and used their wines as a commodity of trade. They incorporated wine into their religious practices, the cults of Bacchus and Dionysus.

The Bible contains many references to wine, and wine has become an important part of the religious ceremonies of many churches. In spite of this, some church groups are very much opposed to all forms of alcohol. This reaction is found primarily in groups that were started on the American frontier and whose first social cause was the elimination of saloons and alcohol along the United States' western borders. These groups eventually were able to get an amendment to the U.S. Constitution prohibiting the sale and manufacture of alcohol. But we are getting ahead of our story, more about Prohibition later.

There are references in the Bible to the use of wine by the Hebrews from the earliest dates. In Deuteronomy 18:4 we read that wine could be used to pay the tithe. The Hebrew wine press with its upper and lower chambers—the upper for crushing the grape, the lower for receiving the juice—is referred to in many Old and New Testament passages. The bursting of wine skins, which indicates that fermentation has taken place and that alcohol is present, can be read about in Matthew 9:17, Mark 2:22, and Luke 5:37.

Romans 14:21 is often used as an argument favoring the prohibition of alcoholic consumption. In reality, the passage does not require abstinence, it simply says that it is fine to abstain if you have such convictions. Indeed, if this passage prohibits drinking wine, then it also prohibits the eating of meat.

There is a Biblical passage that states that you should drink wine. I Timothy 5:23 in the New English Version says, "...take a little wine for your digestion...." The King James Version says, "...use a little wine for thy stomach's sake...."

It was the Romans who spread vineyards throughout

Europe. They took the grape with them on their conquests. Romans regularly used wine for medicinal purposes and by 300 A.D. had planted grapes along the countries of the Northern Mediterranean.

The Romans made a great many advances in the making and storing of wine. They added flavorings to wine and also had additives that would lower or mask its acidity. They stored wine in glass bottles and made special glassware for drinking their wines. During the late Roman period cooperage, the making of barrels, was invented. The water-tight barrels invented by the Romans could hold wine and keep it protected from the harmful air.

The Romans and their accomplishments are akin to the Americans and the revolution they have created since World War II. Fermentation tanks that can be heated and cooled have been invented. These stainless steel tanks have brought the fermentation process under man's total control. Special picking and stemming machines were also introduced in the Americas.

Early wines were generally poor in quality and were undoubtedly drunk soon after fermentation as they would very soon be contaminated by air and turn to vinegar. Water, however, was more likely to be contaminated than wine was. These early wines were probably about the safest drinking liquid in the ancient world. Wine had a nice warming effect in winter and was probably *the* medicine in the ancient world. It was loaded with suspended materials that contained many vitamins and yeast.

After the fall of Rome, in the Middle Ages, the church became the primary tender of Europe's vineyards. The wine produced by these church-maintained vineyards was used by the monks for food and for sacramental purposes in the Mass.

Charlemagne, the Emperor of France around 800 A.D., was a great encouragement to wine growers. French vineyards from the Roman period were maintained and many new vineyards were started.

In 1066 a group of Northern Frenchmen (Normans) conquered England and were later able to gain control of other portions of France including Bordeaux. As a result, wine was introduced into England. The most popular wine in England, claret, is a Bordeaux made from the Cabernet Sauvignon grape.

From about 1100 A.D. to 1300 A.D., European Christians tried unsuccessfully to gain control of the Holy Lands area controlled by Moslems. The contact between these two groups had some distinct advantages for Europeans. Among them was the system of zero or Arabic numerals, which enabled Europeans to rid themselves of the cumbersome Roman numerals. Many new spices were brought back to Europe. Better medical practices in the Eastern Mediterranean were brought to Europe, and, most important to our discussion, new grape varieties were introduced.

It was during the late Middle Ages that wine trading between European countries became well established. During the 1300's and 1400's, international wine trading eventually led to the standardization of wines and winemaking.

All during the 1000 years of the Middle Ages the church was quietly tending its vines. Then, during the French Revolution, church property was broken up and the church vineyards were sold to private individuals. Many of these vineyards are still producing; some of them are the homes of France's highest quality wines.

From the 16th to the 18th century, the rise of the middle class led to a greater and greater demand for wines, and the wine industry began to blossom. By 1850 winemaking and wine consumption were well established and widespread throughout Europe.

Then catastrophe struck. In the latter half of the 19th century many diseases swept through European vineyards. The most damaging work was done by phylloxera. Phylloxera is a plant louse that destroys the roots of the grape plants. As a remedy, the tops of European grapevines were grafted onto American rootstock resistant to the disease. The phylloxera epidemic caused the immigration of many European wine specialists to other parts of the world including, of course, the United States.

Also in the latter half of the 1800's, Louis Pasteur was making major contributions not just to science, but also to the wine industry. He found micro-organisms in wine that thrived when the wine was exposed to air. The growth of these micro-organisms led to the spoilage of the wine. This discovery was the beginning of the scientific revolution in winemaking. Americans have continued this revolution on a far greater scale than have Pasteur's countrymen.

Another tremendous aid to winemaking has been the invention of machinery that has greatly facilitated the picking and crushing of grapes. This mechanical revolution has helped to keep the cost of wine low.

In America, wines have a long history. In 996 Bjarni Herjulfsson was blown off course from his Greenland base by a severe storm. He sighted the east coast of present day Canada and returned to Greenland. An expedition was formed under the leadership of Leif Eriksson, who landed and spent a winter at Newfoundland. The foundations of Viking long houses have been found there. The Vikings tended to name their new lands for their physical appearance. Iceland and Greenland are examples. North America was called Vinland because it was covered with vines. Although this is debated among historians, many are certain that those vines were grape-bearing.

Grapes grew in most parts of North America, and 100 years ago virtually every American city produced wines. The evidence of this was lost when most of these vineyards were uprooted during Prohibition.

Florida gets credit as the place in the United States with the earliest record of winemaking. The Florida wines were made before the New England settlements of 1609 and 1620. These wines were made from the wild grapes that grew abundantly in the area. The first wine made from domestic grapes came about the time of the American Revolution.

Thomas Jefferson once wrote about the need to develop a wine market in the United States. During his lifetime, hard liquor was more commonly drunk than wine. Jefferson said, "No nation is drunken where wine is cheap and none sober where the dearness of wine substitutes ardent spirits as the common beverage."

About the same time John Wesley wrote in his diary, "Wine is one of the noblest cordials in nature." A startling comment in view of the fact that Wesley's followers today are Prohibitionists.

During the first half of the 19th century commercial establishments began to produce wine from grape varieties that had been domesticated.

It was not until mid-century, after the Gold Rush of 1849, that California wines began to go through a period of vast expansion. The expansion was too rapid, however, and much of the grape industry went bust. When the railroad arrived in 1869 it offered an outlet in eastern markets for the overproduction in California.

The latter half of the 19th century saw the beginning of many of California's great vineyards. This was a period when many of the great personalities of the California wine industry were alive.

Charles LeFranc was one of the people who in 1852 started Almaden vineyards. His son-in-law Paul Masson founded, of course, Paul Masson vineyards. He was one of the developers of a California Champagne. Paul Masson vineyards today are among the great premium-wine producers in the United States.

In 1858 Charles Krug founded his winery in the famed Napa Valley. He planted and sold varietal wines. The firm was purchased during World War II by the Mondavis. Robert Mondavi left the family, moved across the road, and now runs another fine California vineyard, Robert Mondavi Wines.

In 1861 Agoston Harazythy went to Europe and brought vine cuttings back to the United States. He planted many vineyards in California and today is known as the "father of California wines."

The German Beringer Brothers founded their California winery in 1876, the nation's centennial year. They are best known for aging their wines in caves.

Inglenook was founded by the Finlander Gustav Niebaum

in 1879. He planted varietal grapes and made varietal wines.

One of the few family vineyards still remaining in family hands is that of Wente Brothers. It makes excellent white and red wines and was founded in 1883.

In 1886 three brothers from Czechoslovakia founded the Korbel Winery. They are most noted for their excellent Champagne.

As is evident from the last few paragraphs, the latter half of the 19th century was a period of great enterprise and expansion in California.

After the completion, in 1869, of the transcontinental railroad, there developed a great deal of competition between the western and the eastern grape growers. Wines made in California were given New York labels and New York wines were labeled to appear that they came from California. Both areas were falsely using French labels. These practices led to legislation of the wine industry. Controls were correctly placed on the labeling and manufacture of wines. These controls were started in the 1890's and were obviously needed.

By the turn of the 20th century California wines were of excellent quality and began to win international prizes. Over the next two decades advances in winemaking further improved California wines.

Then the bottom fell out of the wine industry in the United States—Prohibition.

During Prohibition grapes sold very well as people were making their own wines at home. Some vineyards were allowed to continue to make wines for sacramental purposes. These sacramental wines were used by Catholics and Jews in their religious ceremonies and observances.

Although it took years, California and the other wine-producing areas of the United States were able to recover from Prohibition. In one way, Prohibition was a blessing in disguise because the American wine industry had to rebuild using new and modern equipment for winemaking. The old equipment was sold to foreign markets or destroyed when Prohibition was passed. The new technologies that were employed in the rebuilding gave the United States a real production and quality advantage over the wines of the rest of the world.

There are still many holdovers from Prohibition. Nearly 15 percent of all the counties are still dry today. There are high taxes on all alcoholic beverages. In many states these taxes are used to support public education. What's amazing about that is that until recently many teachers have had to sign oaths that they would not consume intoxicating beverages. The informal pressure is still strong in many areas against alcoholic drinks being consumed by public employees.

Prohibition took its toll not only on the wine industry, but on the publishing industry also. Prohibitionists demanded that references to wine be cut from many of the great classics. Pressure has been placed on schools and libraries to stock no books on alcoholic beverages. A textbook for California school children that discusses agricultural products makes no reference to the wine industry. A Bible has even been published that omitted all references to wine.

After the repeal of Prohibition, a group of ingenious wine merchants and a good advertising campaign made wine known to Americans, and the consumption of wine has increased dramatically since. There was a period of slowdown during World War II so that grapes could be made into food products.

Since World War II, large multi-national conglomerates have been buying up wineries. Since the war years the number of wineries has been reduced by 80 percent. Bigness is taking over.

Since 1960 people and restaurateurs have become more knowledgeable and appreciative of wine.

The decade of the 1970's has become the "golden age of wine." Sales have increased dramatically and dry dinner wine consumption has surpassed sweet dessert wine consumption. The age of wine sophistication has arrived in America.

Chapter Five

A WINE AND CHEESE TASTING PARTY

Harmonious Partners

Wine and cheese have traditionally been considered harmonious partners. Wine and cheese can make a very festive occasion for a group of six people. The following suggestions for a program of wines and cheese will make a delightful party that is easy to do. Six is the best number of people for this kind of party because a wine bottle contains six servings. For twelve people you would have two bottles of each wine.

The first wine served should be a white wine, perhaps one made from Sylvander or Riesling grapes. A nice German Rhine wine would be well suited for this first course; Johanisberger Riesling would also go well. Serve Gouda cheese with this course.

A rosé should be the second wine served, but it should be one that is on the dry side. A Grenache rosé is highly recommended. Serve a Neufchatel or Havarti cheese.

The third wine should be a bottle of Zinfandel or Beaujolais: enter the reds. Serve these wines with a Swiss, Gruyere, or a mild Cheddar cheese.

The fourth movement of this symphony should include a bottle of Cabernet Sauvignon or Bordeaux. Notice how we have moved from a white wine to a rosé to a light red to a heavy red. Serve Brie or Camembert cheese with this fourth course. Let the Brie or Camembert sit at room temperature for about two hours before serving.

The fifth wine to be served should be a White Pinot, a Pinot Chardonnay, or a Pinot Blanc. The cheese for this occasion should be Edam.

The sixth and final course will be a bottle of Pinot noir or Burgundy. Serve with Bleu or Roquefort cheese.

Long loaves of crusty French bread should be served throughout the tasting. If you would like to do some extra work you can make Hot Cheese Balls, Cold Cheese Balls, or Cheese Tarts and serve them with the wines. Recipes follow. You need not serve cheese with each wine, but if you don't you will be missing half the fun. You may wish to serve fruit with the white wine courses.

To help cut the cost of the party, you may want to ask each person to pay one-sixth of the price of the wine and cheese. It is best, however, to have one person buy all the wine and cheese. Then there will be no communication problems, which could result in one of the guests showing up with a wine or cheese that does not fit the planned tasting. Also, if one person buys all the wine he or she may be able to get a discount because you will be purchasing a half-case. The lower price can then be passed along to each of the participants. Finally, no one person will be stuck with having to buy the most expensive wine or piece of cheese.

During the tasting, give each person just one wine glass unless, of course, you have enough glasses to carry you through the evening. Have a pitcher of water and an empty ice bucket at the table. Between wines rinse the glasses and empty the water into the ice bucket.

If your guests bring the wine, be sure to have them chill the whites and rosés ahead of time.

You may develop your own variations of the tasting party. For instance, you might have an all-Cabernet Sauvignon tasting. Buy several bottles of Cabernet, each one from a different vineyard but all of the same year. Then you will be able to tell which vineyard you like best. Or buy Cabernet bottles from the same vineyard but of different years. You will then know whether you prefer your Cabernets young or old. Or buy a couple of French Cabernets (Bordeaux) and a couple of California Cabernets. Do you like domestic or foreign Cabernets the best?

You may like to try a tasting using only one type of wine but several types of the same family of cheese. One interesting cheese variety is the bleus. Buy some bleu, Roquefort, Stilton and Gorgonzola.

Try tasting only sweet white wines. Or taste only dry red wines. Try several different types of wines from the same vineyard. Try a sherry, Madeira, or port tasting. The possibilities are unlimited.

Fruits go nicely with white wines. Try the same fruit with several different white wines. Or try the same wine with several different types of fruit.

Wine tastings are different and exciting. As you taste, take notes on your impressions of each wine—using, of course, the Andersen Wine Tasting Note Card.

Recipes

The following recipes will go well with any or all wine courses.

Cheese Tarts

To make cheese tarts you will need tart tins—approximately 16 small 1¼ inch) or 5 larger (3-inch) tins. If you do not have tart tins you can use a muffin tin.

1. Make your favorite pie-crust dough.
2. Press a small amount of the dough in the bottom and up the sides of each tart tin. If you are using a muffin tin, press the dough in the bottom and ½ inch up the sides of each muffin cup.
3. Cut your favorite cheese into small cubes and place them on the prepared dough.
4. Mix together:
   1 cup of heavy cream
   1 egg
   Worcestershire and Tabasco sauce to taste
5. Fill each tart with the cream mixture.
6. Bake for 15 minutes at 350 degrees Fahrenheit.
7. Serve at room temperature.

Cold Cheese Balls

1. Soften 8 ounces of cream cheese. (Use Camembert or Brie if you prefer.)
2. Mix in 1 teaspoon of white wine.
3. Add and mix in ½ pound (2 sticks or 1 cup) of butter.
4. Refrigerate for several hours until firm.
5. Form into small balls, about ½ to 1 inch in diameter.
6. Roll the balls in finely chopped nutmeats.
7. Refrigerate until firm or until ready to serve.

Hot Cheese Balls

1. Melt 2 tablespoons of butter in a saucepan.
2. Add 4 tablespoons of flour and mix together.
3. Cook for 3 to 5 minutes, stirring frequently.
4. Add 1 cup of milk.
5. Whip with a wire whip or at low speed with mixer until smooth. (You now have a Bechamel sauce.)
6. Simmer until thickened, stirring frequently.
7. Add and mix well:
   - 1 tablespoon of butter
   - 2 eggs, beaten
   - 1 cup of shredded cheese
8. Add your favorite herb or spice to taste. Nutmeg, mace, pepper, tarragon, or sage are especially nice.
9. Form into small balls.
10. Dip in beaten egg and roll in bread crumbs. Repeat.
11. Refrigerate until chilled throughout.
12. Deep fry for 1 to 2 seconds at 400 degrees Fahrenheit.
13. Reheat just before serving in a 350 degree Fahrenheit oven for 3 minutes.

The following bread recipes make excellent accompaniments for wine and cheese.

Italian Bread

1. Combine and gently mix together the following ingredients. Scrape sides of bowl a couple of times.
   - 3 packages dry yeast
   - 4 cups of flour
   - 3¾ cups of 110 degree water
   - 4 teaspoons of salt
2. Beat mixture rapidly for 3 minutes. Use an electric mixer set on high.
3. Add 6½ cups of flour and mix in by hand. Add additional flour if necessary.
4. Knead dough for 15 to 20 minutes and shape into a ball.
5. Let rise until double (about 1½ hours) in a greased and covered bowl.
6. Punch dough down. Re-form into a ball. Let rise again until double.
7. Punch down. Let dough rest for 10 minutes.
8. Grease a baking sheet and sprinkle with cornmeal.
9. Divide dough into thirds. Shape dough into long loaves and place on sheets. Cover, let rise until double in size.
10. Heat oven to 375 degrees and bake for 20 minutes.
11. Brush loaves with 2 lightly beaten eggs to which 2 tablespoons of water have been added.
12. Bake for an additional 20 minutes.
13. Cool on racks.

Bread Sticks

1. Mix together:

    2 cups of flour
    5 teaspoons of sugar
    2 packages dry yeast
    2 teaspoons salt

2. Prepare separately and add to dry ingredients.

    1½ cups of 110 degree water
    ¼ cup of melted shortening or salad oil.

3. Beat ingredients for 5 minutes by hand or for 3 minutes on high setting of an electric mixer.

4. Add another 2 cups of flour and mix in by hand. Add additional flour if necessary.

5. Knead on a lightly floured surface for 5 minutes.

6. Form into a ball, place in a greased bowl and turn ball over so that all of ball gets greased.

7. Cover and refrigerate overnight.

8. For large breadsticks, 4 times the size of a pencil, divide dough into 18 equal parts. For small breadsticks, twice the size of a pencil, divide dough into 36 equal parts.

9. Let divided dough rest for 10 minutes.

10. Roll dough between hands or on a lightly floured surface into long strands about the size of a pencil's diameter for small bread sticks and about twice the size of a pencil's diameter for large breadsticks.

11. Place on greased baking sheets and let rise until doubled in size.

12. Bake at 400 degrees for 10 to 15 minutes.

(continued)

For the wine and cheese toasting party, leave the bread sticks plain as you want to use them to clear your palate between wines. For other occasions, try these variations:

1. After shaping bread sticks but before raising them, sprinkle them with coarse salt or roll in sesame seeds. A light sprinkling of nutmeg is nice. Try rolling the bread sticks in caraway or poppy seeds.

2. During the second step add directly to the dough any of the following herbs: sage, marjoram, rosemary, chervil, tarragon, thyme, parsley, chives or basil.

Tips on Using the Bread Recipes

Read. Read through each recipe before you begin. This will give you a sense of where you are headed with the project. You will also be made familiar with the ingredients you will need.

Microwave. If you own a microwave oven with multiple cooking settings you can raise the dough in one-third to one-half the time required. Place the dough in a well greased bowl. Grease top of dough by turning it over in bowl. Wet a kitchen towel and wring it out. Place towel over top of bowl. Place bowl in microwave oven. Use a non-metallic bowl. Set microwave at lowest setting (preferrably 10 per cent) and warm bread for 3 minutes. Let bread rest for 10 minutes. Repeat until bread is double in size. Should take about 30 to 40 minutes.

If you own a microwave oven with a meat probe, you can heat the water to dissolve the yeast in to exactly 110°. Place water in glass measuring cup. Place meat probe in water. Set oven for 110°

Conventional oven. To raise bread in a conventional oven set temperature setting at lowest possible position. Heat oven. Turn oven off and place bowl containing well greased dough in oven. Be certain to cover bowl with a kitchen towel that has been soaked with water and wrung out. If bread is not rising fast enough turn heat back on for 3 to 5 minutes.

Kneading. Kneading is absolutely essential because it aids the dough in rising and affects the quality of the bread mixture. To knead bread dough, place the ball on a lightly floured surface. Press the palms of your hands into the ball of dough. With the tips of your fingers, pull the dough back over on itself. Repeat the process. As the ends of the dough ball mushroom out, fold them back toward the center. Add flour to surface as needed. Kneading time varies with the bread being made. Some breads should not be kneaded at all. Follow the recipe instructions.

Appendix

Glossary of Terms Commonly Found on Wine Labels

Abboccata (Ah-bo-kah-toe) *Italian*. Semi-sweet.
Amabile (Ah-ma-ba-lay) *Italian*. Sweet.
Amontillado (Ah-mone-tee-yah-doe) *Spanish*. A dry, pale sherry.
Amoroso (Ah-mo-ro-so) *Spanish*. A sherry, dark and sweet.
Anejo (Ahn-yez-ho) *Spanish*. Aged.
Apéritif (Ah-pair-ee-teef) *French*. A before-dinner wine.
Appellation Controlée (Ah-pell-ah-see-awn Con-trol-lay) *French*. Controlled by government standards (See *French Wine Classifications* and *V.D.Q.S.*).
Asciutto (Ah-shoot-toe) *Italian*. Dry.
Auslese (Ouse-lay-zeh) *German*. Moldy, ripe grapes made into an excellent sweet wine.

Basto (Baas-toe) *Spanish*. A common sherry.
Beerenauslese (Bearen-ouse-lay-zeh) *German*. Made from the ripest grapes of a bunch, a sweet white wine.
Bereich *German*. Region of growth. The name of the region is given on the label. (See *Wine Growing Regions of the World)*.
Bianco (Bee-onk-ko) *Italian*. White.
Bulk Process See *Charmat Process*.

Charmat Process. (Shar-mah). A fast, inexpensive way of making Champagne. The Champagne is made in large vats and not in bottles.
Chateaux (Shot-toe) *French*. Castle. The word precedes the name of the place where the grapes are grown.
Chateaux Bottled See *Estate Bottled*.
Clos (Clo) *French*. A vineyard with a wall or fence around it.
Cuvée (Cou-vay). A batch of wine. If you buy and enjoy a wine with a cuvée number, you can return to your wine dealer and buy another bottle with the same cuvée number, reasonably certain that it will be the same. Cuvée is similar to dye lots in the clothing industry.

Demi-sec (Dem-me-seck) *French*. Sweet.

Dessert. Means fortified. It does not necessarily mean sweet.

Dom (Dawm) *French*. A wine made at a cathedral.

Domaine (Doe-main) *French*. Wines made from grapes of a single site and ownership. (Not a mixture of grapes from several owners.)

Doux (Doo) *French*. Sweet.

Dry 1. Not sweet, puckery.
2. Not fortified; that is, less than 15 percent alcohol.

Dulce (Dool-thay) *Spanish*. Sweet.

Echt (Ekt) *German*. No sugar added.

Edel (Eh-dell) *German*. Used as a prefix on some German wine labels; means excellent.

Eglise (A-gleeze) *French*. Church.

Einzellage (Eyn-zell-la-guh) *German*. Wine made from the grapes of one vineyard only, not a mixture.

Eiswein (Ice-vine) *German*. A wine made from frozen grapes.

Eleveur *French*. Shipper.

Estate Bottled. Wine that is bottled at the same place that the grapes were grown and fermented.

In France one of the following phrases must appear on the label:

Mise du Chateau
Mise en Bouteilles au Domaine
Mise du Domaine
Mise au Domaine
Mise en Bouteilles par le Proprietaire
Mise a la Propriete
Mise du Proprietaire

In the United States the term "Estate Bottled" must appear on the label. (See *Produced and Bottled by* and *Made by*.)

Fino (Fee-no) *Spanish*. Type of sherry.

Flor (Floor) *Spanish*. Sherry that gets its flavor from a yeast grown on the surface of the sherry.

Fortified. Wine to which alcohol has been added. In the United States the term "Dessert Wine" is used to denote fortification.

French Wine Classification. The best French wines are grouped into the following classifications:

1. *Grand Cru*
2. *Premier Cru*
3. *Deuxieme Cru*
4. *Cru*
5. *Cru Classe*

These classes were created at an exhibition in 1855 and have not changed since; that is, the wines in each class have never been re-evaluated.

Frizzante (Freez-zahn-tay) *Italian.* Sparkling.

German Wine Classification. The Germans have three wine classifications:

1. *Qualitatswein mit Pradikat* (Kual-ee-tates-vine mit pred-ee-khat)—highest category
2. *Qualitatswein*—quality wine under government control
3. *Tafelwein*—table wine

Grand Ordinaire (Grawnd Or-dee-nair) *French.* A medium-class wine.

Grand Vin (Grawnd Van) *French.* An excellent wine.

Kabinett *German.* Designates an excellent wine, estate bottled and unsugared.

Made by. . . . Means that 10 percent of the wine in the bottle was grown, fermented, and bottled by the vintner whose name appears on the label. (See *Produced and Bottled by* and *Estated Bottled.*)

Madeira. Apertif or dessert wine. There are four types:

1. Sercial—dry
2. Rainwater—medium
3. Bual—sweet
4. Malmsey—very sweet

Manzanilla (Mahn-thahn-neel-ya). Pale, very dry sherry.

Marque Deposee (Mark) *French.* Means the trademark is registered.

Mise (Meeze) *French.* If the label has this word in a phrase, see *Estate Bottled.*

Natur (Nah-tewr) *German*. No sugar added.
Negociant (French). Shipper.

Oloroso (O-lo-ro-so). Sherry: dark, full-bodied, high in alcohol, made without flor yeast and sweet to medium-dry.

Port. A dessert wine, sweet and fortified. There are three types:

1. Ruby—dark, young, and fruity
2. Tawny—light and mellow, aged
3. Tinta—dry, full-bodied

Produced and Bottled by. . . . Means that 75 percent of the wine in the bottle was grown, fermented, and bottled at the vineyard appearing on the label. (See *Made by* and *Estate Bottled.*)
Proprietaire *French*. Owner of the vineyard.

Qualitatswein. See *German Wine Classifications.*
Qualitatswein mit Pradikat. See *German Wine Classifications.*

Rein *German*. Same meaning as *Natur*—no sugar added.
Reserve. An advertising term often found on wine labels; it has no meaning.

Schloss (Sh-lawss) *German*. Castle.
Sec (Seck) *French*. Dry.
Secco (Say-co) *Italian*. Dry.
Sekt (German). Sparkling wine.
Sherry. Six types, all described separately.

1. Amontillado
2. Amoroso
3. Flor
4. Fino
5. Manzanilla
6. Oloroso

Solera (So-lehr-ah). Method of making sherry where many different vintages are blended to make the product that reaches your table.

Spatlese (Shpate-lay-zuh) *German.* Sweet wine made from grapes picked very late in the harvest season.

Tafelwein *German.* Table wine. See *German Wine Classification.*

Trockenbeerenauslese (Trawk-ken-been-en-aus-lay-zuh) *German.* Rare wine made from the best grapes of the bunch, which are shriveled almost to raisins before fermentation.

V.D.Q.S. *French.* Superior wine but not as good as a wine that carries an *Appelation Controlee* designation.

Vermouth. Fortified, flavored white wine. Usually flavored with wormwood, but other herbs and spices are also used.

Vignernon (Veen-yair-rawn) *French.* A man who grows the grapes for wine, winegrower.

Vihno (Veen-ho) *Portugese.* Wine.

Vine (Van) *French.* Wine.

Vine *French.* Fortified.

Vin Ordinaire (Van Or-dee-nair) *French.* Common or lower quality wine.

Viticulteur (Vee-tee-cuhl-ter) *French.* A man who grows grapes, winegrower.

Wein *German.* Wine.

France

Importer
Contents
U.S. REPRESENTATIVES
FREDERICK
WILDMAN
AND SONS
NEW YORK CITY
TABLE WINE
PRODUCE
OF FRANCE
CONTENTS
750 ml
ALCOHOL 11 %
BY VOLUME
1976
1976
Vintage date
BEAU-RIVAGE®
Place where wine is made
BORDEAUX
The growing area
APPELLATION BORDEAUX CONTROLÉE
Wine is bottled under certain controls
MONOPOLE
BORIE-MANOUX
Sélectionné et mis en bouteille par:
BORIE-MANOUX - Négociant à Bordeaux - France
PRODUCT OF FRANCE
Shipper

Germany

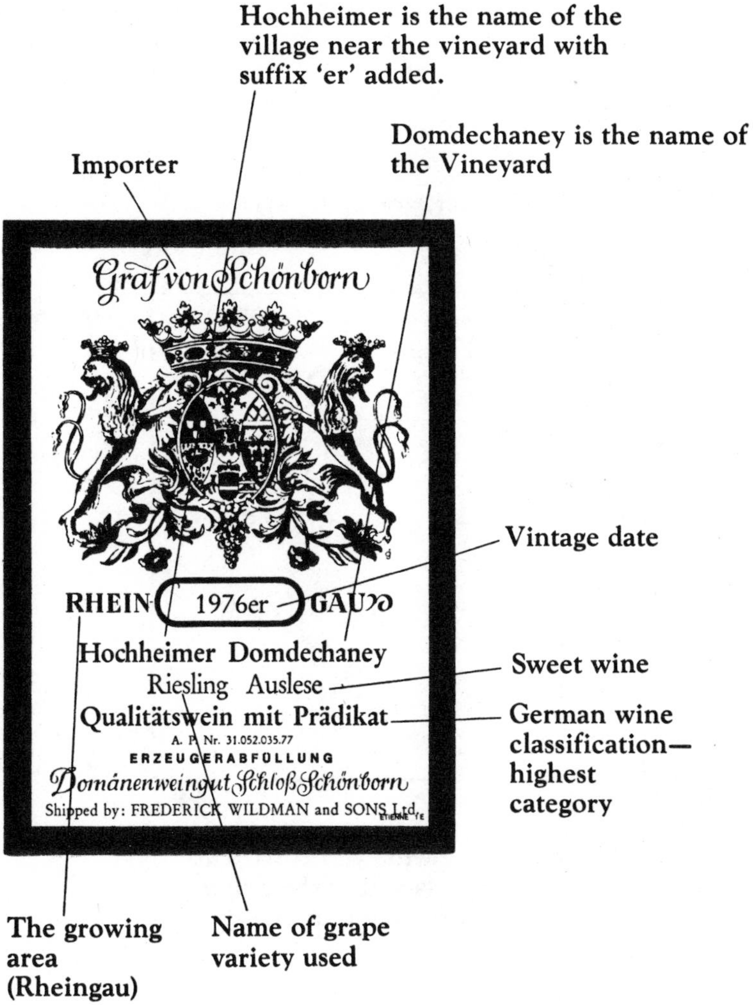

Hochheimer is the name of the village near the vineyard with suffix 'er' added.

Importer

Domdechaney is the name of the Vineyard

Graf von Schönborn

RHEIN 1976er GAU

Hochheimer Domdechaney

Riesling Auslese

Qualitätswein mit Prädikat

A. P. Nr. 31.052.035.77

ERZEUGERABFÜLLUNG

Domänenweingut Schloß Schönborn

Shipped by: FREDERICK WILDMAN and SONS Ltd.

Vintage date

Sweet wine

German wine classification—highest category

The growing area (Rheingau)

Name of grape variety used

California

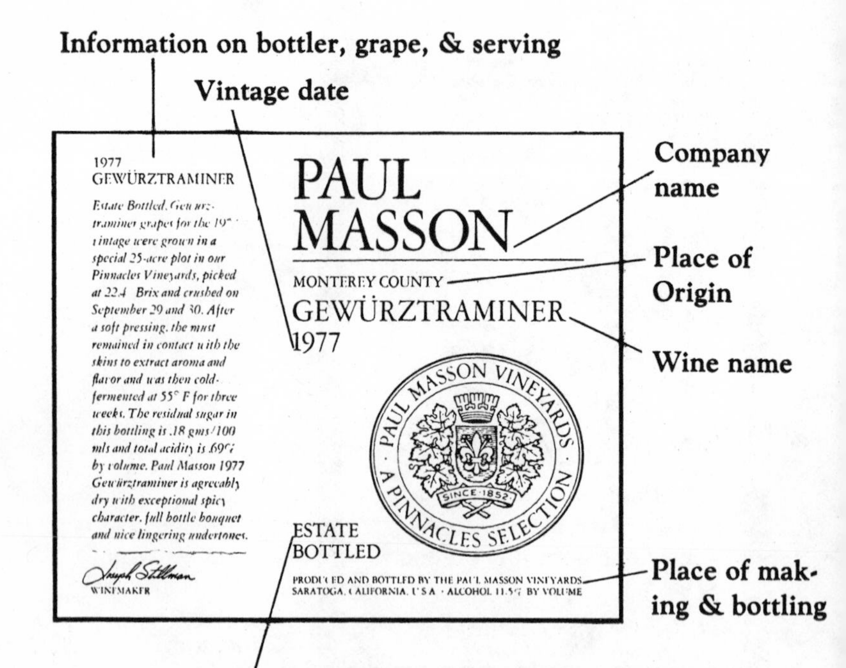

means the wine was bottled at the same place that the grapes were grown & fermented

Wine Growing Regions of the World

A wine label will list both the region and city or village where the wine is grown, produced, or bottled. Listed below are the names of most of the regions of France, Italy, Germany, and the United States that grow grapes for wine.

France

ALSACE
ALOXE-CORTON
ARMAGNAC

BEAUJOLAIS
BEAUNE
BORDEAUX
BROUILLY
BURGUNDY

CALVADOS
CHABLIS
CHALONNAIS
CHAMBOLLE-MUSIGNY
CHAMPAGNE
CHASSAGNE-MONTRACHET
CLOS DE VOUGEOT
COGNAC
COTE DE BEAUNE

FIXIN
FLAGEY-ECHEZEAUX

GEVREY-CHAMBERTIN
GROWES

HAUT MEDOC

LOIRE

MACONNAIS
MEDOC
MEURSAULT
MORAY ST. DENIS
MUSCADET

NUITS ST. GEORGE

POUILLAC
PERNAND VERGELESSES
POMERAL
POMMARD
POUILLY-FUME
POUILLY-MONTRACHET

RHONE

ST. EMILION
ST. ESTEPHE
ST. JULIEN
SAUTERNE
SAVIGNY-LES-BEAUNE

VOSNE-ROMANEE
VOLNAY

Italy

Abruzzi
Apulea

Basilicata

Calabria
Campania

Emilia

Friuli

Lazio
Ligura
Lombardy

Marches
Molise

Piedmont

Sardinia
Sicily

Trentino
Tuscany

Umbria

Val d'Aosta
Veneto

Germany

Ahr

Baden

Franken

Mittle Rhein
Mosel

Nahe

Pfalz

Rheingau
Rheinhessen

Wurttemberg

United States

Almeda—Calif.

Chautauqua—N.Y.
Contra Costa—Calif.

Finger Lakes—N.Y.

Hastings—Minn.

Lake—Calif.
Lodi—Calif.

Mendocino—Calif.

Napa—Calif.

New York
Niagara—N.Y.
North Coast Counties—Calif.

Ohio

Sacramento—Calif.
San Benito—Calif.
Santa Clara—Calif.
Santa Cruz—Calif.
San Joaquin—Calif.
Scuppernong—Southern U.S.
Solano—Calif.
Sonoma—Calif.

Major Wine Growing Areas of Germany

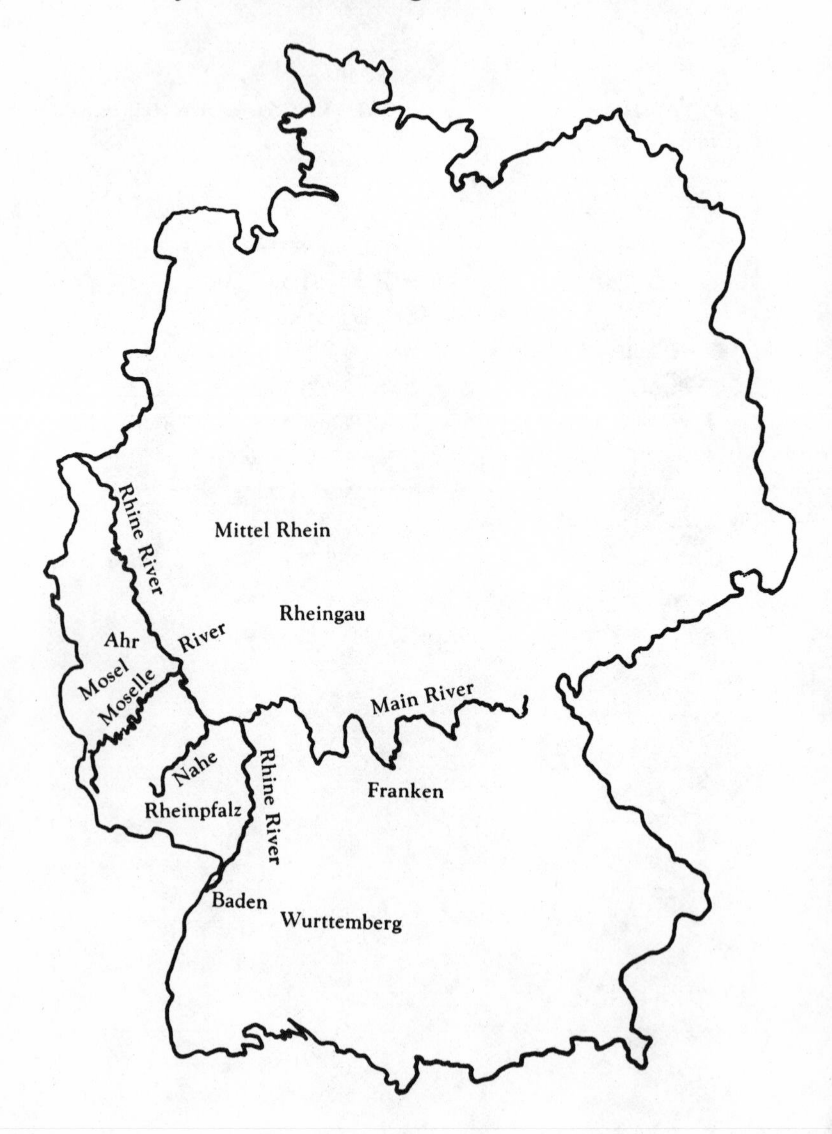

Major Wine Growing Areas of Italy

Major Wine Growing Areas of France

Major Wine Growing Areas of California

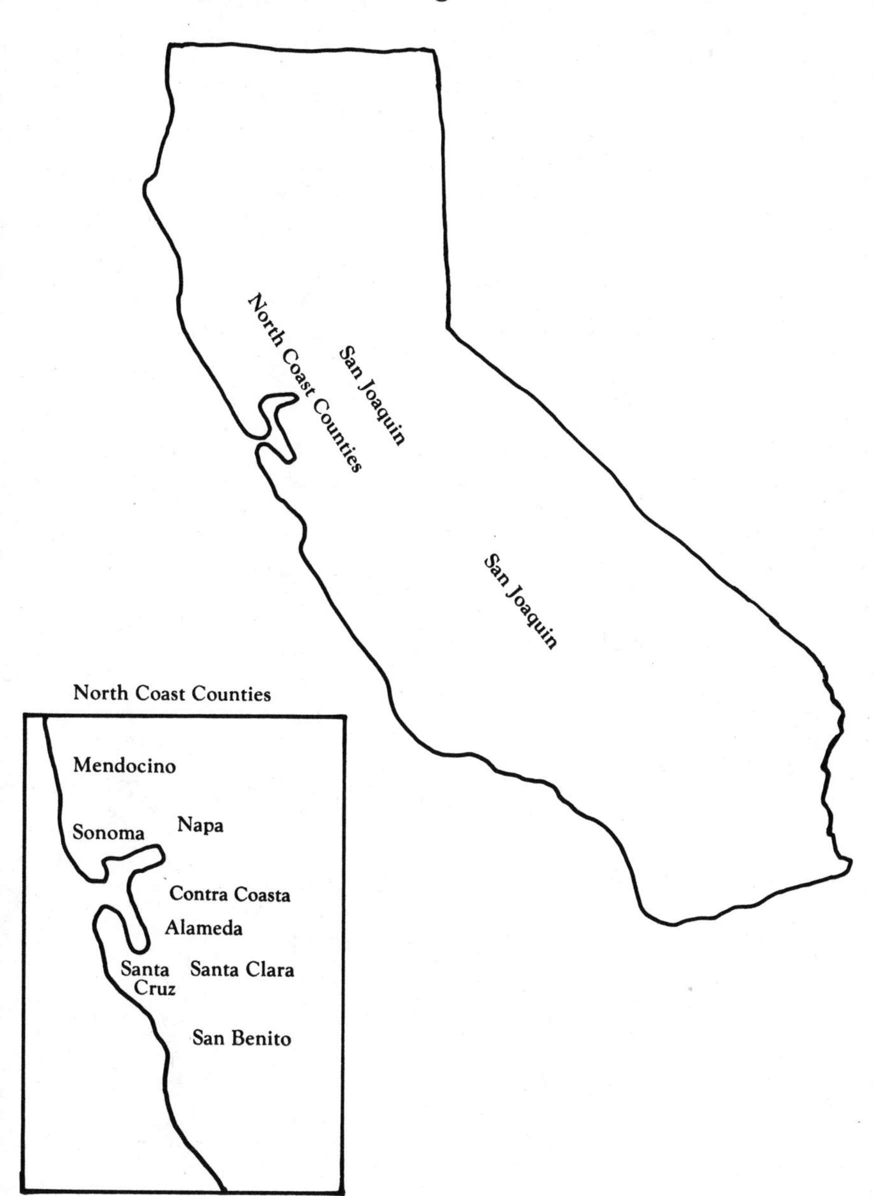

Notes

Notes

Notes

Notes

Notes